THE BEGINNER'S
GUIDE TO
Starseeds

THE BEGINNER'S GUIDE TO
Starseeds

Understanding Star People
and Finding Your Own
Origins in the Stars

Whitney Jefferson Evans

Adams Media
New York London Toronto Sydney New Delhi

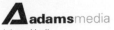

Adams Media
An Imprint of Simon & Schuster, Inc.
100 Technology Center Drive
Stoughton, Massachusetts 02072

First Adams Media hardcover edition January 2021

ADAMS MEDIA and colophon are trademarks of Simon & Schuster.

For information about special discounts for bulk purchases, please contact Simon & Schuster Special Sales at 1-866-506-1949 or business@simonandschuster.com.

The Simon & Schuster Speakers Bureau can bring authors to your live event. For more information or to book an event contact the Simon & Schuster Speakers Bureau at 1-866-248-3049 or visit our website at www.simonspeakers.com.

Interior design by Michelle Kelly
Interior images by Frank Rivera

Manufactured in China

10 9 8 7 6 5 4 3 2

Library of Congress Cataloging-in-Publication Data has been applied for.

ISBN 978-1-5072-1536-4
ISBN 978-1-5072-1537-1 (ebook)

CONTENTS

INTRODUCTION

Starseeds are deeply intelligent and spiritual souls who made a decision to live a lifetime on Earth to help humans raise their collective energetic vibration and otherwise improve life on our planet.

Starseeds are humans, through and through, and they look, act, and talk like anyone else in this world, but they are actually beings who were originally created on other planets and stars. They live many lifetimes all over the universe, but on Earth they are human beings who practice self-love until they become the highly vibrational, encouraging people who motivate other humans to help our planet thrive physically and spiritually. While specific purposes vary from starseed to starseed, some common goals are taking care of our planet, helping anyone who needs assistance, and sharing their positive energy with others.

If you have a feeling deep inside that these goals resonate with you, it's likely you are a starseed yourself! When starseeds are born, they forget everything about their previous lives in order to live a completely human lifetime on Earth, so it's not surprising if you don't remember other lives. You would have grown up like the rest of us and experienced the true struggles of being a three-dimensional person on our planet. Some starseeds live their entire lifetime on Earth never consciously knowing about their star lineage, but this book can help you awaken into the knowledge of your true self. If you are a starseed, this book will help you learn more about who you are, where you came from, and what your purpose is so you can fulfill your incredible destiny to the best of your ability. You will also find quizzes and checklists to help identify your starseed qualities and information on how to get in touch with your star family, should you desire to do so.

In Part 2 of this book, we'll explore the different starseed lineages, such as the Sirians, Pleiadians, and Andromedans (and more!) that are most commonly connected to planet Earth. While all starseeds share certain qualities, their personalities can differ based on their star origin. Learning about each lineage's unique traits can help you identify which lineage you were born into so you can discover your heritage and purpose.

No matter which lineage you come from, your goal as a starseed is to help lift up everyone on Earth to become the best versions of ourselves. *The Beginner's Guide to Starseeds* will show you how to harness the extraordinary qualities and amazing power inside you so you can enrich humanity with love, kindness, and empathy. Being the best version of yourself truly means changing the world!

Part One

What Are Starseeds?

Do you believe there is life outside of Earth? If so, it's not difficult to imagine that human beings would have a connection of some sort to those star beings who live outside of our own planet. Could they even be watching over us, protecting us? You might even believe that some humans on this planet actually have originated from the stars. This book will dive into the phenomenon of starseeds, people who chose to exist on our planet after a previous lifetime in outer space. They are here to raise our collective consciousness for the greater good.

Chapter 1
An Introduction to Starseeds

Renowned American astronomer Carl Sagan once said, "We are all made of star stuff. We are a way for the cosmos to know itself." He is right: Human beings are made from elements of the Earth and the stars—and starseeds are that and more. Starseeds have lived entire lifetimes in other places in outer space and have gained immense knowledge as a result (whether they've realized this fully or not). They have a mission that will burn inside of them like a fire until they realize it. They came to this planet at this exact time in order to help the Earth. Our planet is in disarray at the moment, largely because of the way humans have treated it. Its temperature is rising, its icecaps are melting, and fires are starting all over the planet. Starseeds are here to foster peace and understanding between humans and our environment.

STARSEEDS, DEFINED

Starseeds are souls who are not from our star system or galaxy but have chosen to incarnate on Earth. They have made the conscious decision to come to our planet to help it become the best version of itself—to help the planet and its people ascend to a higher dimension. In essence, starseeds:

- Have deep, personal connections to other stars, planets, or galaxies in the universe.

- Have lived many lives in many different galaxies before this one but have chosen to live a three-dimensional, human experience right now.

- Have strong intuition and psychic abilities—basically their very own superpowers—that help them along the way.

- Are part of an entire galactic family.

- Chose to live on Earth at this exact time in history to help humankind be the best it can be.

These amazing beings walk among us and are as much a part of our world as any other person. Starseeds have zero malicious intentions. They are not here to study us, investigate us, or report back to their home as to what they have seen. They aren't here to shame us or make us feel badly for what's been done to the planet—or ourselves. Starseeds are here—from a star system not our own—to help us become the best versions of ourselves. The name "starseed" implies two truths of their being: one, that they're from the stars, and two, that they're here to "plant a seed," or to help us grow as a planet. While they may be used to living in higher dimensions, starseeds actually want to live on Earth in the third dimension to exist as we do. They want to learn spiritual lessons they cannot obtain where they come from.

Starseeds are here—
from a star system not
our own—to help us
become the best versions
of ourselves.

WHAT DO STARSEEDS LOOK LIKE?

When starseeds are born on Earth, they forget everything about their previous lifetimes, any knowledge they had, and even their mission for Earth. They will grow from babies to children to adults just like the rest of us. Their skin, organs, thoughts, feelings, and actions are the same as anyone else's; the only difference is that they may "wake up" one day to the fact that they are starseeds.

COMMON TRAITS OF STARSEEDS

Starseeds are human beings through and through, and you wouldn't be able to discern them from a regular human being just by looking at them. They look, act, and talk like anyone else in this world. However, there are a number of traits that starseeds share; starseeds:

- Tend to be very empathetic and are able to relate to other people and animals with ease.

- Have totally unique personalities.

- Do not like rules or restrictions.

- Feel passionately about the Earth, the environment, and the animals who live here.

- Are peaceful people who cannot stand conflict.

- Know they have a mission to complete here on Earth, and, despite not always knowing what that mission is, they are extremely purpose-driven.

- Often feel homesick for a place that isn't here on Earth...because their true home is in the stars!

Starseeds and the Skies

Starseeds usually love anything that has to do with outer space, whether it be studying astronomy, reading their horoscope, or just looking up at the night sky. They feel a special connection to and kinship with the cosmos.

STARSEEDS' SPECIAL SKILLS

Starseeds also share some special abilities that allow them to be impactful people on our planet. For example:

- They have an extremely strong sense of intuition. They can sense things will happen before they actually do, and they usually have one or more clairvoyant ability they can tap into.

- They enjoy a variety of psychic skills, like telepathy and other extrasensory abilities.

- Their dreams are incredibly vivid, to the point where they might actually be visiting other worlds, dimensions, or speaking with their intergalactic family in their dreams.

- Starseeds have a keen interest in and understanding of metaphysics based upon the knowledge they obtained in previous star lifetimes.

- They are often some of the most creative people you will ever meet. They are able to use their artistic expression to make bold statements and even channel messages from their star families in the sky.

These talents, interests, and skills enable starseeds to spot areas of need, offer assistance, and share love and hope with others.

WHERE DO STARSEEDS COME FROM?

Starseeds come to Earth from galaxies all across the universe, including our own. Some starseeds originate on planets we've identified and named, while others venture here from galaxies you've only ever dreamed of.

When you start thinking about the universe, its vastness becomes obvious very quickly. Although the outer parts of our galaxy (the Milky Way) seem far away, ours is actually considered to be a small galaxy, relatively speaking, and it's only one of a potentially infinite number of galaxies in the universe. Starseeds can originate from our own or any one of these galaxies, which means they are a diverse and varied group.

The exact star where a starseed comes from is called its star lineage. Some star lineages choose to live on Earth as starseeds more often than others, and each has their own personality traits and strengths.

Common Star Lineages of Starseeds

Following are some of the more common star lineages of Earth's starseeds:

- **Pleiadians** come from the Pleiades star cluster, part of the constellation Taurus. They have a desire to heal those who are broken.

- **Sirians** come from Sirius, the brightest star in our sky, and have been helping those on Earth since the time of ancient Egypt.

- **Orions** are logic-minded people from Orion's Belt and often come here to work on their karma.

- **Andromedans** come from the constellation of the same name and are nomadic, free-spirited types.

- **Lyrans** are born in Lyra, the lyre constellation of the same name, and take on leadership roles.

- **Arcturians** live on Arcturus in the Boötes constellation and are highly intelligent math whizzes.

These are just some of the fascinating star backgrounds we'll get into in more detail later in the book.

MEETING YOUR STAR FAMILY

This book will also teach you how to communicate with your star family. Don't fret: Intergalactic beings aren't going to just drop in on you one day while you're brushing your teeth. They're smart enough to know humans aren't willing to receive them without being called upon first. We'll discuss how to strengthen your intuition in order to communicate with your star family and then go over how to ask them to make contact with you.

STARSEEDS AND THE AGE OF AQUARIUS

If you pay attention to pop culture, you've likely heard of "the Age of Aquarius." It's perhaps best known from the popular 1969 song by the band The 5th Dimension (originally written for and appearing in the hit musical *Hair*). That song also popped up in the final scene of the movie *The 40-Year-Old Virgin,* where Steve Carrell, Catherine Keener, and others wear white and dance around with flowers and joyous expressions. So, we can assume the Age of Aquarius is something the hippies of the 1960s and 1970s talked about, but what does it actually mean?

The Age of Aquarius in Astrological Terms

Astrology is defined as the study and forecasting of events through the observation and interpretation of celestial bodies. In other words, we look at the placements of the stars, Sun, Moon, and planets to discern information about our future. In astrology, the signs are shown in a circle, with Aries considered the beginning, then Taurus, Gemini, Cancer, Leo, Virgo, Libra, Scorpio, Sagittarius, Capricorn, Aquarius, and Pisces. After Pisces, the cycle begins again at Aries. Astrological ages move in the opposite direction (called retrograde) and are defined by the Sun's position during the vernal equinox. Each age is approximately 2,150 years long.

The Age of Aquarius occurs when the Sun's position during the vernal equinox (in March) moves from Pisces to Aquarius. As this happens, Pisces, the last sign of the zodiac, will move in retrograde (or backward) to Aquarius, which comes before it. While we understand the timing of the equinox each year, the exact timing of the Age of Aquarius is unclear. Some astrologers believe the Age of Aquarius began in 2012, based upon the placement of the star Regulus (in the constellation Leo) and how it moved in that year. Others believe we aren't there yet and will have to wait another five hundred years, while others believe we've been in the Age of Aquarius for thousands of years already. Overall, most agree we're either there or will be in the near future.

What Does the Age of Aquarius Mean?

While the exact timing of this new era is widely debated, the impact of it is not. The Age of Aquarius will mark a major turning point in the planet's culture. The key highlights are that humans will:

- **Take better care of the Earth:** People will take control of the planet, realizing their destiny as keepers of the Earth who must take care of it.

- **Experience enlightenment:** It is believed to be a time when human beings will fully awaken and expand their consciousnesses.

- **Find true happiness, fulfillment, and utter peace:** The wars of the world will cease and we will live together in harmony.

- **Share resources:** Everyone will share cooperatively, and your needs will be at your fingertips. Humans will no longer have to struggle.

- **Advance their technology:** In this new high-dimensional state of being, we'll also be able to communicate with other planets and galaxies in the cosmos so we can learn from them. Because of this, it's believed we'll be able to create new species of plants and animals and our technology will advance even faster than it does now.

- **Change their physical makeup:** It is believed we will move from a three-dimensional life to a five-dimensional one and from a carbon-based physical body to a crystalline one.

All of these incredible transformations won't happen overnight—we won't wake up one day and see that the world has changed around us. It's more probable it will happen slowly, with many small changes creating a cumulative effect. Colors may be seen more vibrantly, and people, places, and things will appear more radiant.

The Age of Aquarius will mark a major turning point in the planet's culture.

Starseeds and the Age of Aquarius

So what exactly do starseeds have to do with entering the Age of Aquarius? Starseeds have specifically come to live on our planet as humans to help move us into this new era. Spiritual teachers and folklore suggest that souls have visited other planets throughout time in all sorts of galaxies but that it is only happening on Earth right now. There are many starseeds living here at this time because we are in this transitional period on Earth.

As we'll discuss throughout the book, starseeds have many special qualities to them. They are extremely intuitive beings with a knack for the psychic senses. They have a unique knowledge based on lifetimes of experience that they are here on Earth to impart upon us. Their energy is highly vibrational, meaning they are quite literally emanating good vibes into the world each and every day. They are solely here to help inspire us as humans and guide us to be the best versions of ourselves—and our planet. There's no one better suited to help guide humanity into the Age of Aquarius, and starseeds are ready and willing to do so.

Chapter 2
A Starseed's Mission

Now that you've learned the basics of starseeds, it's time to delve into how they awaken into this knowledge of themselves and why they're visiting Earth at this point in time. Once awakened, starseeds go through a process of self-healing and self-actualization. They will need to truly embrace themselves and practice intense self-love. They learn more about themselves through meditation, creative endeavors, or traumatic events. No matter how they come into the knowledge that they are starseeds, their lives will be forever different—in the best way possible—and they will see the world around them as a much more vibrant and happier place.

HOW YOU MIGHT FIGURE OUT YOU'RE A STARSEED

You can come into the knowledge that you are a starseed in many different ways. Here are some of the most common.

Via Media or Word of Mouth

The same print or online media where you get your news and entertainment might open your eyes to your starseed nature. You may read an article about them, watch a video online that includes them, or notice some mentions of them on a message board. Maybe you heard someone talking about starseeds—after all, word of mouth is a time-honored way of spreading information. Maybe you saw this book and felt a twinge of recognition and just felt curious about the subject matter. If you felt drawn to this topic in any way, it's highly probable you may be a starseed yourself.

A Traumatic Event

Not every starseed learns of their lineage on the Internet or by a friend sending them a link. Many starseeds are "awoken" into this knowledge through some kind of life-defining experience. For example, traumatic events have a way of triggering this information in people. Accidents, the death of loved ones, extreme stress, and nervous breakdowns are all examples of occasions in your life that can open you up to this realization. Times of crisis cause human beings to make radical shifts in their life, and this can open up energetic space to learn about your star lineage.

During a Near-Death Experience

Relatedly, there have been many instances of people who have near-death experiences who learn about their star lineage in that way. It's believed they may have learned about their star lineage while they were unconscious or "on the other side." Some people have woken up with the knowledge inside them, while others recall actually speaking to someone while they were "out"—their higher self, ancestors, guides, or their star relatives—who told them about it.

Through Meditation

Another way of coming into this knowledge is through meditation and other spiritual pursuits. Meditation is a method of clearing your mind to create a sense of peace and overall well-being. When your mind is not busy focusing on stress and random thoughts throughout the day, it's free to receive information from higher sources. There have been many starseeds who have learned of their star lineage in this way. It usually will happen to someone who meditates regularly and is able to sit for long periods of time without distraction.

By Creative Expression

It's also possible to awaken to the knowledge that you are a starseed through creative expression. Starseeds are extremely artistic and creative people and, as such, they have talents in the arts: painting, sculpting, dancing, singing, drawing—you name it. These arts have a meditative effect, meaning your mind and body can relax into a receiving state while you're engaged in them. This allows for information to pop into your head while you work, and the message that you are a starseed can be passed along this way.

You Are Born Knowing It

There are some lucky starseeds who have been aware of their star lineage since birth. This, of course, is quite rare and astonishing in nature. These individuals are highly spiritual people. They'll often know exactly what they want to do on this planet and spend their entire lives executing their goals.

You May Never Find Out

Some starseeds never actually learn about their star lineage. Since starseeds are human beings like the rest of us, there's often no reason for them to wonder or question where they are truly from. It's been suggested that only around 10 to 20 percent of starseeds will actually come to realize their true nature during their lifetime. While it may seem like a "missed opportunity," we must also realize that everyone is on their own path and it is still possible to shift the Earth's energy for the better without consciously knowing you are a starseed. There are many ways to leave your impact on the Earth, and learning about your star lineage is only one of them. In fact, many starseeds who do not know of their true background are still drawn to healing, lightwork, artistic expression, and other commonly shared starseed traits—meaning the result of their efforts in their lifetime would be the same or similar to those who have knowledge of their lineage.

WHAT HAPPENS AFTER YOU DISCOVER YOU'RE A STARSEED

When you awaken into your starseed lineage, you will start to see the world through entirely different eyes. A sense of clarity will appear in your life and you'll find that you:

- Can now answer many questions you had about yourself.

- Have a new idea of what's important to you—and what's not.

- Start to appreciate the beauty in everything around you.

- Understand certain aspects of your personality that coincide with this new knowledge.

- Can look back at certain events in your lifetime with new understanding.

- Begin to utilize psychic and intuitive skills that you may not have even realized you had. (Much more on the psychic abilities of starseeds later.)

When you realize you're a starseed, you will likely embark on a journey of self-healing and self-love. After all, in order to help others, you must first heal yourself. A broken person cannot truly assist in the healing of someone else until they have worked on their own issues. As this process happens, starseeds will attempt to recall as much information about their previous lives as possible.

STARSEEDS' MISSION

Starseeds are here on Earth for a very specific reason: to raise the energetic vibration of the planet in order to improve the quality of life here. They're here to help us fix what's out of whack and correct our path to the future. They want to assist us all in living the best lives we possibly can on our space rock in the middle of the universe. Thanks to their special skills, they are able to:

- Bring their light to the places on Earth that need it, helping human beings, who tend to fall into darkness with ease.

- Support other people as they learn to love themselves.

- Share their powerful energy all across the globe.

- Aid anyone and anything needing assistance.

- Encourage the planet to become the best version of itself.

Let's look a little deeper into two key elements of the starseeds' mission: helping the Earth and supporting people as they discover self-love.

Starseeds are here on Earth for a very specific reason: to raise the energetic vibration of the planet in order to improve the quality of life here.

Helping the Planet

Taking care of the Earth is a vital part of a starseed's mission. They may spend time actively working with the Earth's energy, cleansing and purifying it and casting the darkness from it. They stand up for the Earth and urge people to tend to it. This could mean a starseed spends time:

- Working with activists to help prevent climate change.

- Protesting turning a national park into a drilling site.

- Calling elected officials to explain why our natural resources are worth protecting.

- Educating others about what's going on with the planet right now and why it's so important to act quickly.

They are probably quite vocal about their views and may use public speaking engagements or social media to make them heard. They do not worry about antagonizing others with their views because they are confident in their mission and what's at stake. Because they have lived lives in galaxies that are much more advanced than ours, they know how harmonious life on a planet can be. They will do everything in their power to help humans enjoy that sort of peace.

Mother Gaia's Hopes for Earth

According to those who have communicated with star beings, spirit guides, and the planet itself, Mother Gaia has set a specific intention to raise the vibration of planet Earth. She is well aware of the damage being done to the planet and of the nature of human beings at this period in time. She has set a goal to ascend, as a planet, into the fifth dimension and for humanity to become more crystalline. Starseeds are here to help her on her mission to make the planet truly shine.

Encouraging Self-Love

Starseeds have a passion for helping others shine brightly and live their lives authentically and with passion; to find joy in everything they see, feel, and do; to live such a happy, brilliant life on this planet that their energy and light are infectious. That's where the magic happens.

You see, there is a ripple effect from a starseed who is living their authentic truth. When you exist as the best version of yourself, you have the best experience possible during your time here on Earth. Nothing pleases your soul more than living your best life, and when you shine brightly, you inspire others to do so as well. Every day that you speak your truth and share it with the world, you are connecting with other people who will take what you say to heart. When you live your life this way, you stop living a life of self-criticism and doubt and open yourself up to the needs of others and the world as a whole. As such, you'll free up time to do charitable (and heroic) acts, which benefit others and the community as a whole. Living this lifestyle is something others can look up to and inspire to do one day. This happens through your relationships too. It's entirely possible that seeing you become the best version of yourself will spark others—friends, family, colleagues, and anyone you make contact with in this life—to look inward and work on themselves. That's how starseeds affect such amazing change on Earth.

THE LIFE CYCLE OF A STARSEED

The life cycle of a starseed can vary greatly depending on when someone actually discovers their star lineage.

Phase 1: A Soul's Decision

The first part of a starseed's life cycle is actually being born on this planet. Before their lives begin, a starseed's soul makes a decision to incarnate on Earth. When starseeds are born, they forget everything they knew before: their previous lifetimes, their knowledge, and their actual mission here on Earth. If you're wondering why this happens—and that's a good question—it's because their soul agreed to a fully human experience. To be human is to live a human life, to learn as you go. If you were born with all sorts of innate knowledge, you would not be having the same human existence as everyone else. Starseeds must fully integrate into Earth's three-dimensional way of being.

Born Anew

While it *is* possible to be born with the knowledge that you are a starseed, knowing exactly what you're going to do in your lifetime, it is very rare. The majority of starseeds live their first few decades of life with no knowledge of their star lineage. This not only helps them relate to other humans; it also allows them to think, see, and feel like them.

In order to make an impact on other people, it's important for starseeds to know how humans operate. "Starting over" also teaches starseeds soul lessons they wouldn't learn elsewhere. We all know that times of struggle generally help us in some way, whether by learning important lessons or adding life experience. When starseeds are in this first cycle of life, they may feel alone, depressed, or unworthy. They often don't feel like they have value or can't see that they someday will. They have major issues trusting other people and often cannot trust themselves. They're searching for answers, and the longer they search, the more helpless they may feel. They tend to feel homesick for somewhere other than their actual home. They often feel like the world isn't fair, that they're a victim of circumstance or just plain unlucky. Sometimes they'll act out and hurt others, or even go on a path of self-destruction and hurt themselves. These common conflicts appear in many (but not all) starseeds and can drive a person to deep despair or a full-on breakdown. Luckily, their true selves are usually waiting on the other side of this darkness.

Phase 2: Awakening and Healing

The next part of a starseed's life cycle is their awakening. When starseeds learn of their star lineage and star family, it can be an incredibly reassuring feeling. Difficult parts of their lives begin to make more sense when they look back at them with this new knowledge. Their entire perspective changes. What once may have seemed hopeless now suddenly feels just fine. They begin to see the Earth as a wonderful home for plants and animals and to really appreciate nature. Some starseeds have even reported that they see color more vibrantly after this awakening.

When starseeds learn of their star lineage and star family, it can be an incredibly reassuring feeling.

In this part of their cycle, starseeds embark on a phase of self-healing. As mentioned earlier, for a starseed to truly shine, they first need to heal themselves fully. In this phase, they'll work on learning to love themselves. They'll also experience love for all beings and come into the understanding that we are all one. This grasp of unity and oneness will help put all their previous struggles into perspective. They'll work on strengthening their connection to their heart and harnessing this power for good.

Phase 3: Fulfilling Their Mission

Once this level of self-love has been achieved, the next part of a starseed's life cycle is the era of embracing their star lineage. Now that they know what their gifts are, they aren't afraid to pass them along to others. They spend time helping others, the planet, and themselves. They are completely aligned internally, having lost all of their inner struggle. They can fully express themselves without any reservations and speak the honest truth. They dedicate their time to causes that will improve the planet for all who live on it. They share their gifts with everyone around them and have an infectious goodness to them that people can't ignore. They inspire others to become better versions of themselves, which in turn helps with the goal of raising the Earth's vibration. They may even work together with other starseeds in a large group to raise the consciousness of beings across the universe. Overall, this is a very joyous and peaceful existence that anyone would be lucky to have.

Learning to Love Yourself

The path to living as the best version of yourself is not always an easy one. Human beings are born into a society that projects unrealistic ideals onto all of us—and it's really hard to shake them. We're constantly being bombarded with magazines that tell us how we should look, TV shows that reinforce stereotypes, movies that make heroes out of people who should never be seen as icons, and memes that are self-deprecating, causing us to downplay our best characteristics instead of letting them shine. Thankfully, we're living in a time when things are changing—so accept and embrace yourself for who you are!

This is easier said than done, of course. Self-love is a hard thing to come by for most of us. We're usually not taught to spend time getting to know ourselves—our real selves—and we suffer for it. Women especially are taught to provide for others and help anyone else before helping themselves. We are all deserving of love, especially love for ourselves. It's not worth your time to look in the mirror and wonder why you don't look the same as the people you see all over the media. Instead, look at the world spiritually, with the knowledge of your starseed lineage in your pocket, and you'll begin to realize that the fleshy human body you're in is just a vessel for your soul here on Earth. Nothing matters more in this life than your own journey of finding your true self—and that begins with loving yourself.

If you relate to this on a personal level—and many starseeds do—there are specific practices you can do to engage in more self-love:

1. **Come up with a mantra, a phrase you repeat over and over with the goal of causing a specific outcome.** The mantra should be something about loving, caring for, respecting, or even just liking yourself. A sample mantra could be "I love myself," "I am happy

living in my body," or "I'm awesome." Write something in your own words that you won't find cheesy and can repeat to yourself whenever you start to feel down. The more you say it, the more you'll believe it.

2. **Write down a list of characteristics you like about yourself.** This may be challenging at first but will get easier as the list goes on. These traits don't need to be awe-inspiring qualities that would blow someone's mind; they just need to be parts of yourself that you like—your infectious laugh, how your legs carry you as you walk down the street, the way your freckles line your face, your dry sense of humor, how easily you remember lyrics to a song, or the fact that you can run a mile without stopping. It can be anything and it can be everything. When you've finished your list, keep it nearby. You may want to look at it on days when you're not feeling at your best.

3. **Write yourself encouraging notes.** Write down some of the qualities you just brainstormed on little pieces of paper or sticky notes and place them where you're likely to find them (in a wallet, book, etc.). Some people have seen great success just by writing "you're awesome" or "you're amazing" on notes and sticking them to their mirror. It's an easy reminder to take a moment to appreciate yourself and why you're actually great. If putting them around your home physically isn't discreet enough for you, you could try sending yourself an email with a similar message or setting a reminder on your phone that simply says "you rock." Take this general idea and mold it into a regular practice that works for you.

4. **Practice gratitude.** There are a number of rituals you can choose from, but the easiest and most effective way to practice gratitude is to simply list things you are thankful for. You can do this out loud, in your head, or you can write them down. It may sound silly at first, but you'll find that once you move on from the major things in your life—like having a roof over your head, food to eat, and friends and family you love—you'll start listing pretty much everything. You can be thankful for anything—nothing is too small. Try thinking about the gifts you've been given, warm meals you've cooked, funny texts you've been sent, small wins in your job, vacations you've taken, and people you've met. You'll come to realize you have so much to be thankful for that it will change your outlook on the world. Some people do this every night before they fall asleep and/or every morning when they wake up so they can fall asleep more easily (and happily) and/or start their day with full hearts.

With a little practice, you, too, can come to find self-love and shine as brightly as you're able.

Phase 4:
Death

Finally, a starseed will experience death, just like the rest of humanity. Upon their death, their soul can choose their next experience. For example:

- They may choose to live their next life back on Earth. This may be because they feel they have unfinished business on the planet or they may have fallen in love with our planet and simply want to experience life as a human once again.

- They could also decide to train other souls to come to Earth as starseeds based on their newly gained experience.

- They could choose to work on ascending to a higher level, whether that's becoming an angel, a guide, or an ascended master of sorts.

- They may want to go back and live their lives on their home planets, where their previous friends and family are.

- They may decide to explore the galaxy further as an intergalactic adventurer.

Death for a starseed can be completely natural or a choice their higher self makes. Many believe starseeds sign a contract to come to Earth and will check in with their higher selves throughout their lives to see how things are going. In rare circumstances, a starseed may choose to exit their contract early via communicating with their higher self or star family in dreams. This may be because they feel their goal has been achieved or they may think they want to "start over." In these instances, a physical death is experienced, though it is not done *to* oneself. After all, these communications are happening between your higher self and the cosmos, not your human ego mind. Following their human death, the soul decides if they want to try again on Earth or live a different kind of life.

It's important to note that the majority of starseeds lead long, full, and healthy lives spent learning, growing, and enacting change around them. Let's learn now about some of the key traits that enable starseeds to be such powerful forces of change on Earth.

Chapter 3
Shared Traits of Starseeds

Now that you have an understanding of who, exactly, starseeds are and why they're on Earth at this moment in history, it's time to learn about certain traits that are common among them. In general, starseeds are highly sensitive people who pick up on the emotions of others and can read the energy of a room as soon as they walk into it. They're extremely unique, creative beings who seem to share a certain longing for their home in the stars. Let's dive in!

EMPATHY

One of the most common shared traits among starseeds is that of empathy, or being able to sense the emotions of others. Empathetic people can easily relate to others on a basic human level.

In Friendships

Being able to understand people and connect to them with ease allows for friendships to form quickly. Starseeds tend to be inquisitive in conversation, as they are genuinely interested in learning about the lives of other humans on Earth and people's experiences beyond their own. Their soul has a desire to soak up its surroundings and learn as much as possible about Earth and its people during this lifetime.

When Listening

A starseed's empathetic nature also means they're highly skilled listeners. They ask questions they truly want to know the answers to, then listen with the intention of learning something new. Their engaging facial expressions and welcoming eye contact act as encouraging nonverbal cues that allow the speaker to feel comfortable around them. Their comforted state combined with a shared empathy means starseeds tend to attract plenty of like-minded people into their circle and often have a lot of friends.

With Animals

The empathetic nature of starseeds generally leads to an affinity for animals, who love them right back. Starseeds may notice that dogs, birds, chipmunks, and more will run right up to them at the park. There's something that connects star beings with the animal world—perhaps it's the true love of being on Earth and appreciating all of its earthly beings, or maybe it has to do with the high vibrations they give off in the world, which in turn attract the animal kingdom to them. Whatever the true reason, starseeds easily connect with animals, which is why they often own lots of pets.

Empathy vs. Empaths

While empathy is a shared trait of those originating from the cosmos, not every starseed is necessarily an empath. Empaths, whether they're conscious of it or not, are people who take relating to others to a spectacular level. They tend to become fully consumed with the emotions and feelings of others, going so far as to cry when others are crying, even if they have no connection to the inciting sad event. Without knowing about and being able to control their empathic nature, empaths can be completely ruled by the thoughts, emotions, and feelings of others. They are overwhelmed in crowds, easily drained of energy, and can sometimes be drawn to a solitary lifestyle due to these extreme emotions. If you're an empath, the good news is that there are plenty of tricks to keep your own energy high and block any unwanted psychic energies from controlling your life.

HOMESICKNESS

Another shared trait of starseeds is a feeling of homesickness, of longing for a home that's not on this planet. This feeling may be hard to express or identify. In fact, you may have felt this emotion but not realized it was a trait you had until reading this just now. This feeling of homesickness for the stars can manifest in a few different ways. It can feel like:

- A constant search for something feeling like home that is never satisfied.

- You don't belong in your community or society as a whole.

- A gut feeling that, no matter where you look, nowhere will feel like home.

Starseeds feel this way because, deep down inside, their soul is homesick for their original home among the stars. Their higher selves know that the town, state, or even country they live in isn't their true "home." To find it, they must look to the stars. In fact, you might find starseeds gazing at the night sky from time to time, a place where they often feel a sense of familiarity.

Unfortunately, this homesickness can manifest as loneliness or even depression at times. Some starseeds spend their lives moving from location to location, hoping they'll eventually find a place that feels like home. This can sometimes come at the expense of their friendships and relationships, or even cause their significant others or families to resent them for being dragged all over the place in a never-ending search for something they won't necessarily find. However, learning about their starseed background can be truly comforting because then they'll finally understand why they feel the way they do. This discovery can be the solution to their sadness.

CHAFE AGAINST RESTRICTIONS

Just imagine the life and times of cosmic beings living their lives in outer space. They have the ultimate freedom! They are not held to the same three-dimensional restrictions humans are born into and, as such, their perception of space and time is different than ours. Their infinite wisdom is incredibly vast and the technology they can access is more complex than the human mind can comprehend. Their lives are lived in ways we can only dream of.

Because of this, it shouldn't be too surprising to learn that another shared trait of starseeds is they don't like having restrictions placed on them. Going from having the entire universe at your fingertips in one soul's incarnation to being restricted to a human body living under human rules in another can be a difficult transition. We can relate to this on a human level too. Have you ever moved out of your family's house, then had to move back in for the summer, a family trip, or in order to save money to buy your own place? When you return to where your parents reside, they often treat you as you used to be: younger, less wise, and less experienced. You find this incredibly frustrating and either rebel against their rules completely or learn to despise them.

Starseeds can be frustrated by a range of the limitations on Earth—including something as basic as the restrictions of the human body (*"Wait, you can't fly here?"*). They tend to be a bit clumsy because they aren't used to this type of body. They may take longer than others to learn a new physical skill because they aren't used to having to work so many muscles and bones to make something happen. They haven't necessarily lived multiple lives on this planet, so they're really trying to get a handle on how everything works.

Starseeds have also been known to have a distaste for the rules of society. They aren't used to being told they can't do something, so it's hard for them to recognize authority. In extreme cases, some starseeds will recede from society and live in the middle of nowhere, where they feel they can live a less restricted life. Usually they are all at least slightly rebellious.

LOVE ANIMALS

Starseeds seem to have an immense affinity for animals. Maybe it's because, where they're originally from, all forms of sentient life are respected and given the opportunity to live full lives. Starseeds see all life-forms as intelligent beings and believe they should be treated the same as humans. They can see through the idea that people are superior to animals and cannot stand that we, as a whole, see ourselves this way. They hate to see animals treated cruelly and have been known to adopt or take in animals in need of a home. In fact, starseeds can be adoptive animal parents to a variety of creatures, opening their homes to as many beings as they can hold. They have a distaste for keeping animals captive and using them for food—starseeds are often vegetarians or vegans for this reason.

Starseeds see all life-forms as intelligent beings and believe they should be treated the same as humans.

Beyond the care and treatment of animals, starseeds also have an unspoken bond with them. They have an indescribable understanding of animals, and animals understand them as well. In fact, many pets and animals are attracted to the positive energy and high vibration starseeds give off. It's not unheard of for someone's pet to joyously chase after a starseed or for a squirrel to barrel over to them just to look at them. Starseeds' empathy helps them understand a lot of what animals are feeling, and, as their skills grow, they may even be able to communicate with them—but more on that in Chapter 4.

ENVIRONMENTALISM

Starseeds are likely to be found educating others on climate change or protesting the latest government rollback on environmental protections. Why, you ask? Because starseeds are very likely to be champions of environmental causes. They incarnated on Earth to help the planet become the best possible version of itself. As such, nothing hurts more than seeing damage done to it. Remember, they chose to live on this planet at this exact time in order to help save the Earth and push our consciousness to the next level.

Considering that starseeds are here to improve life on Earth, it makes sense they would be outraged when certain environmental protections on the planet they love are rolled back. They can't stand it when governments allow the most beautiful natural sanctuaries on Earth to be bulldozed for profit. They lend their voice to a range of causes that protect and care for the planet and its inhabitants.

They also, of course, love to grow life from seeds or seedlings. Starseeds have been known to grow beautiful functioning gardens or to live entirely off the land. They love to grow their own food if they have the space to do so and can develop a green thumb very quickly. City-dwelling starseeds often have an urban jungle of a different sort inside their homes, with plenty of potted plants and herbs growing on their windowsills.

Starseeds are champions of all things eco-friendly in the material realm as well, from the clothes they wear to the items they purchase in stores. They're usually found with water bottles made of glass or metal and never with any single-use plastics. They love to reuse items and can often be found in a thrift store or haggling with someone on *Craigslist* to find what they need. Overall, they'll do anything they can to help Mother Earth—even if it's considered a bit unusual.

UNIQUENESS

Another trait all starseeds share is being unique, truly one-of-a-kind people. Call it being a free spirit or doing things their own way, but all starseeds have this trait in common. Their hearts are in the right place and they're here to complete their mission; they just might not fit society's idea of an average person. But starseeds are best off appreciating themselves for who they really are and not trying to "fit in" anyway.

That is easier said than done, though, and starseeds do often struggle with feeling like outsiders. The truth is they feel different from other people because they *are* different. Being social can be difficult for them, so they may choose to stay home rather than go out. They often make a couple close friends and don't bother expanding that small, trusted circle. To them, it's not worth being dismissed, laughed at, or questioned. Others become homebodies but build a thriving social life online, where they can more easily choose a community they feel comfortable with. Some starseeds, on the other hand, find the real world so difficult to handle that they become shut-ins.

However, many starseeds aren't bothered by feeling different and can be very social beings, choosing instead to own the qualities that set them apart.

Living Your Truth

If you want to work on living your true starseed nature, work on self-love by using the tips in Chapter 2. With a little self-love, you can progress from self-hatred to rocking your personality. Your brightness may be hard for others to embrace, especially those who don't like to see others so happy, but don't let anyone rain on your parade. Keep being authentically you.

FEEL AN AFFINITY FOR THE COSMOS

You know the feeling you have when your school, hometown, state, or country excels in some way and is featured on the news? You likely feel proud inside because it's representative of your roots, your upbringing, and the environment of which you are a product. Now imagine that same feeling, but toward the stars—that's how starseeds feel. Starseeds have a strong tie to space and all things related to it because it's their true home.

Academics

This connection can manifest itself in many ways, but the main channel is through schooling and academic studies. Some starseeds may begin to awaken to their past when they first learn about the solar system, Sun, Moon, and stars in their earliest years of school. This can ignite a spark that leads them to learning even more about these celestial bodies—and themselves.

Astrology

Many starseeds are interested in astrology. After all, the zodiac system is based entirely on the planetary system and the position of the stars. This connection to the cosmos makes astrology truly enjoyable for starseeds to learn about. In astrology, your chart is essentially a "snapshot" of the stars at the exact time you were born. This is why, when making a chart, an astrologer needs your date and time of birth, as well as the exact location where you were born. Starseeds find this mapping of the galaxy at their time of birth to be incredibly interesting and may go on to learn a lot about astrology, perhaps even how to map their own astrological chart.

A Starseed's Curriculum

Once a starseed is old enough to choose their classes or what they'll major in, they may decide to select an area of study that's related to outer space. Astronomy—the study of objects outside the Earth's atmosphere—is a perfect example. These courses talk in depth about planets, galaxies, stars, comets, and other celestial bodies. It's kind of ironic, when you think about it—starseeds learning about where they came from and, in previous lives, had infinite knowledge of. These studies can provide context for starseeds and spark full, visual flashbacks for them.

Astronomy isn't the only area of study starseeds are drawn to. All areas of science are particularly appealing to starseeds (remember their allegiance to the Earth and environmentalism), so they're often interested in subjects like:

- Geology
- Biology
- Chemistry
- Ecology
- Biochemistry
- Zoology
- Geophysics (the study of Earth's physical processes)
- Quantum mechanics (the study of the motion and interaction of subatomic particles; essentially a study of how the universe works at the atomic and subatomic levels)
- Astrophysics (the study of the birth, life, and death of stars, planets, and all other objects in the universe)
- Cosmology (the study of the origins and nature of the universe)

Stargazing

Another way this cosmic affinity can manifest itself is as a general interest in outer space. Many starseeds:

- Stargaze frequently. They might study the stars in the sky to the point where they can tell the difference between a bright, sparkling star and an actual planet. They might also seem to know every constellation that exists.

- Visit planetariums and science museums.

- Have a strong tie to either the Sun or the Moon. For example, tracking the phases of the Moon and how they affect Earth.

- Are fascinated with—or even work for—NASA, SpaceX, To the Stars Academy, or other organizations traveling to or otherwise studying outer space.

PURPOSE-DRIVEN

Another shared trait of starseeds is a strong desire to succeed. There is always a very strong fire that burns inside a starseed! This is because their soul is very goal-oriented. Since their soul has a specific mission at heart—whether that person has awakened to it yet or not—they have a certain inner motivation.

This trait reveals itself in a multitude of ways:

- It can be as simple as starting projects and always finishing them.

- It can show up as a competitive nature, with starseeds always wanting to be the best.

- It can mean working really, really hard on their goals and never giving up.

However a starseed manifests this trait, they always push themselves to do their best—and they usually succeed.

PEACEMAKERS

No matter the situation, starseeds are peace-loving beings. The reason for this is believed to be because so many starseeds come from war-torn homelands. We'll go deeper into the history of many of the star lineages in Part 2 of this book, but for now you can imagine the mindset of someone who has seen bloodshed, suffering, and their homes destroyed because of war. Just like anyone on Earth who has lived through the same trauma, they wish all disagreements could come to a diplomatic rather than military solution. (Could this be the reason the phrase "We come in peace" is so often used by extraterrestrial beings in Hollywood films?)

Similarly, starseeds also bring peace to their everyday lives through their relationships. They have a very low tolerance for getting into disagreements with their loved ones. They know that every being in the universe is connected, so it's stressful for them to see others fighting. Starseeds tend to step in and try to diffuse situations that are boiling over. Watching disagreements blow up and friendships fall apart hurts them emotionally (that's their empathy at play), so they'll do anything they can to fix the situation. They are quite talented at mediating disagreements and are great at helping people get along with each other.

They are quite talented at mediating disagreements and are great at helping people get along with each other.

SEEING THESE TRAITS WITHIN YOURSELF

Have you noticed any of these characteristics in yourself? You may relate to some of these traits but not all of them, or maybe you relate to just one of the listed characteristics. You may not have related to any of these before you picked up this book but now you're starting to notice them in yourself. Or you may have these traits inside but they have yet to be developed, like little parts of your personality waiting in the wings to be utilized. You may also be unsure if you relate to certain traits and can therefore try cultivating them in yourself or if you're more likely to notice them in others. Now that you have this knowledge, you're sure to see these traits pop up all over the place going forward.

Chapter 4
Unique Abilities of Starseeds

From performing something called lightwork to having intuitive abilities, starseeds have specific shared capabilities that set them apart from other humans. Their high vibration allows them to have access to psychic skills like telepathy, manifestation, and clairvoyance. These special skills are imparted upon starseeds to help them during their journey on planet Earth. Read on to see which of these skills you might possess.

STRONG INTUITION

Have you ever felt in your gut that something was wrong with a friend or loved one and then called them only to discover that they really did need some help in that moment? Have you ever dreamed about an event happening and then it actually did occur shortly thereafter? Have you ever walked into a room and sensed something was off, only to discover that something harrowing recently happened there? Have you ever walked away from a job or an experience just because it didn't feel right, only to be validated later? These are just a few examples of intuition, and, if harnessed properly, it can guide you out of harm's way throughout your lives.

Intuition is the ability to know or understand something without reasoning or rationale. You can also think of this phenomenon as interpreting "feelings over facts." This unconscious knowing allows you to perceive the unperceivable and know what you shouldn't inherently know.

How to Strengthen Your Intuition

All starseeds are born with extremely strong intuition, but it's entirely possible you don't have a strong connection to yours if it's been buried, stagnant, or untapped over the years. Luckily, there are plenty of ways to strengthen your intuition.

1. **Learn how to trust yourself.** The more you listen to your inner vision and trust what those gut feelings are telling you, the more you'll be rewarded. An easy way to prove to yourself that you know what's best for you is to write down your feelings and intuitions. This way, you can look back and track your predictions and prove to yourself that you really do know what you're talking about. Journaling is an excellent way to do this, or you may try using tarot or oracle cards and similarly writing down everything you experience to see if your readings come true.

2. **Meditate to connect with your intuition.** When you're able to clear your mind of the daily barrage of thoughts, feelings, and stresses, it allows you to tap into your inner wisdom. Have you ever noticed that you'll come up with your best ideas while you're in the shower, doing a mundane task, or falling asleep? These are all times when your mind is at ease and not bogged down with everyday anxieties or thoughts. When you meditate, your mind has the same clarity and it might just surface some truly interesting insights. Plus, the more you meditate, the better your mind will respond to stress, allowing it to focus on other things—like guiding you with your intuition.

3. **Work with your third eye chakra.** In the chakra system (a network of energy channels in the body that are punctuated by spinning

circles of energy), the third eye chakra controls your intuition. This energy vortex is located on your brow bone, right above and between your eyes. Tapping into this chakra is extremely helpful for strengthening your intuition. You can meditate with this intention in mind, do yoga to help open it up, wear clothing that is indigo in color, or repeat affirmations like "I hear my intuition and trust it is guiding me to my highest purpose." You can also use crystals that are blue or purple in color either to meditate with or to place directly on the chakra. Amethyst, lapis lazuli, sodalite, labradorite, fluorite, azurite, blue calcite, and angelite are all great stones to start with that will help focus your intuition.

CLAIRVOYANCE

Starseeds are highly likely to have clairvoyant abilities. Clairvoyance is the ability to intuitively see things that aren't necessarily there. This is referred to as psychic seeing, psychic sight, or "seeing" with your third or mind's eye. If you can conjure up images in your mind when you're reading a book or imagining something, that's an example of using your mind's eye. This is an ability we all have in us, but most people in modern society either have no knowledge of it or no sense of how to harness it. Starseeds are innately suited to clairvoyance because they would have used this skill freely in previous lives outside of Earth. Because their souls have communicated in this way before, they tend to be born with the same abilities, though they may not be known to the person until discovered later in life.

Other "Clairs"

There are other "Clairs" you might relate to as well:

- Clairsentience is the ability to sense feelings intuitively, or to read the energy of a person, place, or thing.

- Clairaudience is the ability to hear things intuitively, or hear sounds only you can hear.

- Claircognizance is the ability to know things without understanding why you know them.

- Clairtangency is the ability of intuitive touch, or picking up an object and knowing things about it based solely on feeling it.

- Clairalience is the ability to smell intuitively.

- Clairgustance is the ability to taste intuitively.

Everyone has strength in some of these areas and not others, but you may be lucky and experience them all. Just know that we all receive information in different ways, and however you experience clairvoyance is perfect for you.

PSYCHIC SKILLS

Beyond clairvoyance and strong intuition, there's an abundance of other psychic abilities that many starseeds have a good handle on. Because they operate at a higher vibration, they are uniquely able to tune into specific frequencies that the average person cannot. But despite having access to these abilities, they might not be conscious of or have activated them yet. As you read on, see if any of these skills resonate with you. You might already be using some of them without even realizing it.

Seeing or Feeling Auras

Another psychic skill starseeds can tap into is seeing energy and auras. An aura is the emanation of energy around a person's body. An experienced psychic (whether a starseed or not) can see not only the color of someone's aura but also the energy streams within it. They can see holes in the aura, areas that need tending to, or parts that are damaged. Different colors of an aura can reflect a person's mood, their physical health, and the events going on in their life, in the present as well as the distant past and future. They also loosely tie in to the themes of the chakra system. For example, a red aura can indicate that a person is grounded and passionate, while a green aura is representative of love, healing, or being a healer. Overall, the auric field is a clear indicator of a person's energy that can be used to diagnose the inner workings of the mind, spirit, and body. Some starseeds are born with this ability, some grow out of it with age, while others have no experience with it and must learn how to tap into it.

Beyond auras, many starseeds can see energy passing through the human body as well. They're able to see each of the chakra points on the body and can tell you if they're healthy, underactive, or overactive. Their strong connection to energy allows them to put these skills to good use, ensuring people are happy and healthy.

Past-Life Memories

Starseeds often have an innate ability to tap into past-life memories. Some are able to access these previous experiences easily, while others may need past-life regression guidance or deep meditation to get there. Once they have seen or learned about their past life or lives, they open up a well of knowledge that will continue to offer insight throughout their lifetime. These memories often hold the keys to past-life traumas they may still be carrying. Learning about these traumas can help resolve them once and for all. Starseeds may be accessing memories of previous lives here on Earth, or they may be remembering lives lived on other planets. All the information they recall will serve them on their journey.

Manifestation

Another area of psychic abilities for starseeds is manifestation. If you've ever looked back on something and realized you "got exactly what you wanted," well, it's likely you made it happen through manifestation (whether consciously or not). Manifestation is simply the process of harnessing your intentions and energy and directing them toward a goal that you then make a reality. Starseeds are so good at manifesting what they want in life that they often don't understand they're doing it. This is because starseeds have such high vibrational energy that it doesn't take them very long to get what they want. There are many methods of manifesting intentions, but for starseeds, oftentimes just putting their wants into the universe can be enough to make them happen.

Manifestation is simply the process of harnessing your intentions and energy and directing them toward a goal that you then make a reality.

Dowsing and Scrying

Starseeds usually show a great aptitude with psychic tools. For example, they are easily able to use a pendulum for dowsing. Pendulums work by connecting a swinging pendant or weight with a person's higher self to answer a question. The pendant is held in one position and will begin to sway in different directions to indicate a "yes" or "no" answer. When you're holding a pendulum to receive an answer, the answers provided are essentially from your own inner wisdom. When using a pendulum to seek answers, it works best when you're able to connect with it energetically. Since starseeds have a high vibration and can easily connect to their intuition, using this tool is an easy way to make decisions and know that you're getting true answers.

This ability also extends to connecting with the vibrations of crystals, gemstones, and minerals. The process of using these stones to look into the future is called scrying. Starseeds are often able to scry accurately thanks to their powerful energy.

TELEPATHY

Yet another unique ability of starseeds is telepathy, or being able to communicate through the mind or other means not of the five senses. This extrasensory perception (or ESP) occurs when a human can "pick up" on what another person is thinking. (There have been many reports of telepathy between animals and humans too.) This invisible communication is something starseeds can tap into quite easily at times. It isn't used for anything malicious, though it can be helpful in times of distress. This extrasensory way of communicating is believed to be one of the ways intergalactic beings speak to each other, so it makes sense that a starseed would have this skill.

Starseeds Often Use Channeling

Starseeds know human beings aren't necessarily open to seeing or receiving information from star beings, so they often use channeling as a method of reaching us. Channeling occurs when a human is able to clear their mind and receive messages from another source, such as a spirit, ancestor, spirit guide, star being, etc. In this case, these beings "travel" to the consciousness of a human in order to deliver their messages.

For example, consider how twins or multiples (triplets, quadruplets, etc.) often know what the other is thinking or feeling. In fact, many twins have reported that they are able to tap into how their sibling is doing from across the country. This is considered telepathy, even though society often brushes it off as "a twin thing."

Many non-multiples already use telepathy without even realizing it. When you're able to "check in" on your loved ones mentally or through their energy, you are already using telepathy, even if you don't call it that. Part of why this isn't a more widely celebrated ability is the belief that some will use it for evil. Additionally, the powerful people in our societies don't want us to know about our special abilities. Thus, telepathy will likely be laughed off by most, but it's something starseeds are able to tap into with practice.

INTENSE AND
ENLIGHTENING DREAMS

If you've ever had wild dreams where you feel like you're traveling to far-off worlds, it's likely you have a special starseed ability to travel or gain knowledge while you sleep.

Vivid Dreams

Starseeds have been known to experience animated, expressive dreams that can make it feel like they're visiting an entirely different planet—and the truth isn't that far off! It's believed starseeds have the unique ability to travel to different worlds via interdimensional travel while they sleep. In fact, starseeds have reported having all sorts of visions and travels during their slumber. Some have said they traveled to their home planet in dreams, spending time looking at their old familiar places and catching up with their star families. Others say they're able to communicate with higher beings in this dreamlike state and can update them about the goings-on in their life here on Earth. Still others have said they can also communicate with their higher selves in dreams, allowing them to receive information that will help them on their earthly journey.

A common experience shared among starseeds who find them-selves experiencing such vivid dreams is that they wake up between the hours of 2 a.m. and 4 a.m. It's believed that, given the intense dreams and that they often involve astral travel, sometimes our human bodies need a break, and so they wake themselves up from these dreams. If you wake up and remember the dream you just had, lucky you! You can write it down in a journal or spend time recalling the experience you just had. If you can't remember the dream—and many of us won't—rest assured that your higher self has still retained whatever knowledge you received.

Intuitive Dreams

When starseeds are in their dreamstates, they are able to receive information that is helpful to their lives in some way. They might even have precognitive dreams, where they predict something that will happen in the future. Starseeds who have not yet mastered their intuition will receive many of their "downloads" in this way. In these dreams, you may see specific scenes playing out, or you may be told about something that will happen by someone in the dream. These are great reasons to keep a dream journal—you can go back and compare what happened in your dreams to what happened in real life.

Intuitive dreams are filled with information and metaphors for your everyday life. These dreams are meant to gift you with knowledge and advice that will help you with your earthly pursuits. Sometimes the messages in these dreams are very obvious, but quite often they are more of a vague metaphor you are left to decipher upon waking.

Lucid Dreams

Finally, starseeds tend to experience lucid dreams, or dreams in which you're aware that you're dreaming. These dreams are often quite powerful and can even include visits from your spirit guides, ancestors, and other high vibrational beings. In these dreams, try to ask questions you'd like answers to, then take in as much of your surroundings as possible. Again, when you wake, make sure to write it all down!

LIGHTWORKERS

Most starseeds are also lightworkers, which are beings who chose to come to Earth at this time to help transmute the dark into light. Lightworkers are extremely caring and giving individuals who are motivated to make the world a better place for us all and to increase the vibration of the people and planet as a whole. The lives of lightworkers can be as varied as there are countries on Earth, but their goal remains the same: to help raise the vibration of the Earth. Starseeds have the exact same mission, so it's no surprise they are considered to be lightworkers too. Not every lightworker, however, has lived previous lifetimes in other galaxies, so they are not all considered starseeds.

Lightworkers are here to help bring us into a brand-new world, but they cannot do that without helping themselves first. In fact, it is not possible for lightworkers to shine without first healing themselves. Many lightworkers had very traumatic, dark, or humbling experiences while they were growing up and may still be working through the emotional scars from that time. However, they are of no use to the world until they heal themselves.

Once they've worked hard on themselves and healed their emotional traumas, they are able to shine their light outside of their body and share it with the universe. They start with their inner circle first, healing generational traumas and family drama that may have plagued their lives for years. From there, they may wish to help friends and colleagues with their problems. Eventually, these lightworkers will give themselves to the world at large and anyone who needs them.

INTEREST IN AND UNDERSTANDING OF METAPHYSICS

Another unique trait of starseeds is their interest in and ability to understand metaphysics. Metaphysics is a branch of philosophy that looks at the nature of existence and our understanding of it. Aristotle called metaphysics the "first philosophy" and suggested it was the study of the "first causes and the principles of things." This is because, at its core, metaphysics looks at why we are here and why our reality is—or seems to be—the way it is.

While we don't get into the nitty-gritty of metaphysics in this book, we can look at some of the biggest questions it poses to understand why starseeds are drawn to its study. For example, metaphysics:

- Looks at existence, the nature of being (both physical and mental), and how things change (or are perceived to change).

- Seeks to define consciousness and explain exactly why it works the way it does. It also looks at universal sciences (what we all believe to be true).

- Questions space and time and how they are relative, both to each other and to their observer.

- Examines religion, spirituality, and the Divine.

Metaphysics covers a range of topics that are of interest to a starseed!

CREATIVITY

If there's one trait all starseeds share, it's that they are incredibly creative beings. Their creativity can be seen everywhere in their lives but it specifically manifests itself through art. Given their high vibration, starseeds are easily able to access their creativity and to be inspired. Starseeds find great relaxation through working with their hands, singing, playing instruments, and other creative endeavors.

Starseeds, as we know, are extremely driven people, and this desire can be seen through their creative works. They are consistent with their work and a project rarely goes unfinished. They also use their art to express themselves: how they feel inside, how they feel about the world around them, and how they would like to see the world change.

Beyond the art itself, the act of creating is powerful for starseeds. While working, they are transported to a calm, clearheaded place where they can tap into source energy. This energy can be the spark of their creativity or even help guide what they make. However they choose to use their creative gifts, starseeds are all extremely talented.

Given their high vibration, starseeds are easily able to access their creativity and to be inspired.

QUIZ: ARE YOU A STARSEED?

Instructions: Choose an answer for each of the following questions. If you're stuck between two answers, pick the one you gravitated toward first. Keep track of your answers by circling the appropriate bubble. Add up your points according to the answer key at the end of the quiz to see your result!

1. Which word best describes your personality?

   Ⓐ Outgoing **Ⓑ** Introverted **Ⓒ** Unique

2. How often do you look up at the stars?

   Ⓐ Daily **Ⓑ** Sometimes **Ⓒ** Not very often

3. What are your dreams like at night?

   Ⓐ Pretty boring and mundane **Ⓑ** Extremely vivid and mystical
   Ⓒ I don't remember them at all

4. Are you empathetic toward other people and situations?

   Ⓐ Yes, always **Ⓑ** Sometimes **Ⓒ** Never

5. What do you generally do in arguments?

   Ⓐ Sit back and listen **Ⓑ** Dominate the conversation
   Ⓒ Anything that will end the argument

6. How often do you feel lonely and/or isolated?

A Always **B** Sometimes **C** Never

7. How do you feel about outer space?

A I don't care too much **B** It's cool/pretty/interesting
C I'm completely fascinated by it

8. Have you had any psychic or clairvoyant experiences?

A Yes, many **B** Maybe; I'm not sure **C** No, none

9. Do you ever feel like you don't belong?

A Sometimes **B** All the time **C** Never

10. How do you feel about animals?

A I like them **B** I don't care for them **C** I really, really love them

11. What's your preferred genre of entertainment?

A Comedy **B** Science fiction **C** Drama

12. How often do you find yourself daydreaming?

A Always **B** Sometimes **C** Rarely

13. Do you feel homesick often?

A Not really **B** Sometimes **C** Yes, all the time

14.   Have you studied metaphysics before?

Ⓐ Yes, I know all about it   **Ⓑ** I'm familiar but not an expert   **Ⓒ** No

15.   Which of the following is most important to you?

Ⓐ Your safety   **Ⓑ** Your happiness   **Ⓒ** Your freedom

16.   When you were a child, did you have a hard time fitting in?

Ⓐ Always   **Ⓑ** Sometimes   **Ⓒ** Never

17.   How many pets do you have?

Ⓐ 0-2   **Ⓑ** 3-5   **Ⓒ** 5+

18.   Do you feel like you have a mission to fulfill in your life?

Ⓐ Yes, absolutely   **Ⓑ** Maybe, maybe not   **Ⓒ** No, not really

19.   Do other people's actions confuse or completely mystify you?

Ⓐ Yes   **Ⓑ** Sometimes   **Ⓒ** Rarely

20.   Has anyone ever called you an "old soul"?

Ⓐ I don't think so   **Ⓑ** Maybe once or twice   **Ⓒ** Actually, all the time

Answer Key

Question 1: **A** = 1 point, **B** = 2 points, **C** = 3 points
Question 2: **A** = 3 points, **B** = 2 points, **C** = 1 point
Question 3: **A** = 2 points, **B** = 3 points, **C** = 1 point
Question 4: **A** = 3 points, **B** = 2 points, **C** = 1 point
Question 5: **A** = 2 points, **B** = 1 point, **C** = 3 points
Question 6: **A** = 3 points, **B** = 2 points, **C** = 1 point
Question 7: **A** = 1 point, **B** = 2 points, **C** = 3 points
Question 8: **A** = 3 points, **B** = 2 points, **C** = 1 point
Question 9: **A** = 2 points, **B** = 3 points, **C** = 1 point
Question 10: **A** = 2 points, **B** = 1 point, **C** = 3 points
Question 11: **A** = 2 points, **B** = 3 points, **C** = 1 point
Question 12: **A** = 3 points, **B** = 2 points, **C** = 1 point
Question 13: **A** = 1 point, **B** = 2 points, **C** = 3 points
Question 14: **A** = 3 points, **B** = 2 points, **C** = 1 point
Question 15: **A** = 2 points, **B** = 1 point, **C** = 3 points
Question 16: **A** = 3 points, **B** = 2 points, **C** = 1 point
Question 17: **A** = 1 point, **B** = 2 points, **C** = 3 points
Question 18: **A** = 3 points, **B** = 2 points, **C** = 1 point
Question 19: **A** = 3 points, **B** = 2 points, **C** = 1 point
Question 20: **A** = 1 point, **B** = 2 points, **C** = 3 points

Definitely a Starseed
(46 to 60 total points)

Congratulations, you are most likely a starseed! From the answers you provided, it's clear you have quite a lot of qualities typical of starseeds! You're a highly empathetic being and can connect easily with other people and animals. Despite how your friends and family might see you, you know deep down that you don't totally belong in the same way as everyone else. You're an old soul who spends a lot of time daydreaming—and there's nothing wrong with that! It's very likely you chose to live on Earth at this exact time to help shift the global consciousness forward.

Probably a Starseed (36 to 45 total points)

Based on the answers you chose, you are probably a starseed! You share many of the same qualities as starseeds. You may feel lonely or disconnected from the rest of society at times, and that's entirely normal for starseeds. It's possible you feel a deep longing or homesickness inside of you that you can't quite place—this could be your soul's longing for your true home in outer space! You probably have an interest in science fiction movies, TV, and books and can't help staring up at the night sky, wondering what's in the great beyond.

You Could Be a Starseed (20 to 35 total points)

Based on your answers to the questions provided, it's hard to say for sure if you're a starseed or not. You may have chosen answers that are true for you at this time in your life but that could change in the future. You might also be a starseed who has so fully embodied this earthly dimension that you actually don't share the same traits as other self-identified starseeds. Whatever your result, this book will take you through all the different traits of starseeds (and how they differ based upon where they originate) so you can get a clearer idea of whether or not you're a true starseed!

Part Two

Star Families

In this part of the book, we'll begin to explore the different worlds and star families that exist in outer space. While the possibilities are limitless, there are a specific set of star lineages that are common among starseeds on Earth. We'll explore what makes each of them different, and take a look at the star systems that exist within the Milky Way—and beyond.

Chapter 5
Introduction to Star Families

It is important to realize that we, as humans, are not the only sentient life-forms in the universe. There are hundreds of billions of planets and galaxies across the universe, and most of them haven't even been discovered yet. In Part 2 of this book, we'll take a look at our own galaxy, our nearby star neighbors, and the most common lineages of star descent. But first, we'll go through an overview of our own solar system and galaxy and take a look at the universe and its many dimensions.

OVERVIEW OF OUR SOLAR SYSTEM, GALAXY, AND UNIVERSE

As you know, Earth revolves around the Sun, just like the rest of the planets in our solar system. Our home planet is believed to be approximately 4.5 billion years old. Earth is part of the Milky Way galaxy, a twisting, turning spiral with a diameter of more than 100,000 light-years that's home to 200 to 400 billion stars.

The Milky Way is always expanding and is just one of a near-infinite number of galaxies in the universe. The Milky Way is actually part of a large cluster of more than one hundred galaxies called the Virgo Supercluster, a structure held together by gravity. This supercluster has a diameter of approximately 100 million light-years, and all of its galaxies move in their own unique patterns, patterns we still don't fully comprehend.

A Vast Cosmos

From Earth, we have observed trillions of stars and billions of galaxies—and that's only what we can see from our point of view in the universe. The true number of planets, stars, and galaxies is almost impossible to imagine. The possibilities are limitless.

WHERE STARSEEDS HAIL FROM

There are thousands—if not hundreds of thousands or more—star families throughout the universe. Some lineages have arrived from far-off galaxies and settled here while others are just visiting.

Common Stars

When we talk about starseed lineages on Earth, there are a few that are the most common. We'll discuss each in their own dedicated chapter in this part:

- The Pleiadians have the most in common with humans and are seen as our "star cousins."

- Sirians hail from the brightest star in our sky, Sirius, and have shared their alchemy and metaphysical learnings with the rest of the galaxy.

- Andromedans are "free spirit" types who work on breaking down unjust systems throughout the universe, including on Earth.

- The Lyrans are some of the oldest star lineages we know of and are said to be the source of all human beings.

- Orions are logical thinkers who are constantly seeking out the reasons for why things are the way they are.

- Arcturians are strong, powerful healers and encoders of light.

While much of what happens on their home planets remains a mystery to us, we do understand that many of these beings from outer space dedicate a lot of time to helping Earth ascend to the next level. Unlike what so many movies and TV series suggest, our skies aren't full of nefarious beings who want to harm people or our planet. It's entirely the opposite!

Understanding Starseeds' Past Lives

Starseeds have lived many lives before being born on Earth. This very concept is one that some people question, and that's understandable. In order to accept it, you need to be at peace with several ideas. First, you must believe in reincarnation, the belief that souls live multiple lives, perpetually living, dying, and being reborn in a cycle. (This is a controversial spiritual concept that some religions embrace and others refute.) Then you need to acknowledge that some of these past lives may have been lived on another planet in another solar system or galaxy. It's a lot to take in!

Starseeds have lived
many lives before being
born on Earth.

However, many people hear this and immediately know deep inside that it's all true. Some starseeds are awakened by this knowledge that starseeds are born into and live many lives in various locations. Others will have a longer journey to get there but will reap the benefits of this knowledge just the same.

The Basis of All Life: Energy

When talking about these past, present, or future lives, we must also recognize that everything is made of energy. This is a strong foundation to the theory as to why (or how) our souls live on after they've parted with our human bodies. After death on Earth, we exist in a purely energetic state that can eventually decide to incarnate again. Many humans will reincarnate back onto Earth to live another three-dimensional, human life here.

However, if they've evolved enough during their human lifetimes, others may choose to live their next lives somewhere else. If they've completed their missions or learned all they can on Earth, some humans will eventually "graduate" to a higher-dimensional way of living. It's believed by many that the "next step up" from Earth is the Pleiades, where beings exist within the third and ninth dimensions. However, many starseeds have origins in much farther away or more advanced places across the galaxy and might move back to them once they feel they've served the needs of humanity or learned the lessons their soul needed to on Earth.

Understanding Different Dimensions

What does it mean when we speak about different dimensions, on Earth or elsewhere? At its most basic, a dimension is how we perceive reality. On Earth, we live a three-dimensional experience. The way we perceive reality is by the three dimensions we use to measure everything: length, width, and depth. However, scientists believe there are actually many more dimensions than what we know and see.

Time

Time is often referred to as the fourth dimension, meaning it's another way in which we can measure and move through reality. However, humans cannot move in whatever direction they choose in this dimension—we can only move forward in time.

Parallel Universes

How do dimensions differ from the idea of parallel universes? Well, they don't actually differ that much! The idea behind a parallel universe is that it exists outside of our own dimension and we must travel to these alternate planes of reality through a dimension other than our own. Some argue that the idea of alternate or parallel universes is actually just humans experiencing other dimensions. It's believed humans can sometimes visit these dimensions during dreams or even consciously through meditation or other spiritual pursuits.

Superstring Theory

Superstring theory is a theoretical framework that seeks to define all forces of nature through models of vibrations occurring on tiny symmetrical strings. This theory tells us that there are at least ten different dimensions—the three we know, time, and these:

- The **fifth dimension**, which is not too different from our own. If we could see it with our own eyes, we would see the same world around us, just slightly different. It is a more highly vibrational and crystalline way of being. In the fifth dimension, time is not linear and can be experienced as different arrangements.

- The **sixth dimension** is where we are able to see other possible worlds. These worlds start the same but change in different ways in each variation of the world.

- The **seventh dimension** is similar in that you can see other possible worlds, but in this case, they start out very different from each other.

- The **eighth dimension** allows us to see the potential histories of each universe as they branch out into infinite possibilities. These are good examples of the multiverse.

- The **ninth dimension** allows you to compare all the histories of every universe.

- The **tenth dimension** is where anything and everything is possible.

Some scientists even believe there are an infinite number of dimensions, so you can just imagine what the future may hold!

STARSEEDS' CONNECTION TO THE COSMOS

All of these concepts about space, time, and dimensions are important for you to know as it relates to being a starseed. It's important to know they hail from a variety of different places and dimensions across our universe. They are made of energy, just like you and me. They tend to live their lives in cycles similar to that of humans and can have past lives just as we can. This quick introduction to our galaxy and space at large barely scratches the surface of the infinite amount of information that exists. While reading this overview, you may find that certain pieces of information ring true for you or feel familiar. That in and of itself is a sign you could be a starseed.

QUIZ: WHICH STAR LINEAGE DO YOU ALIGN WITH?

Before you learn about the most common star lineages, take this quiz. Read through each section, checking off the boxes that resonate with you. Tally up your totals for each section, then see which section has the *most* checkmarks—that's the star lineage you are most connected to! Keep in mind you might have multiple or strong influences from other star lineages, so it's a good idea to read more about all of them.

CHECKLIST A

Read each of the following statements. Check the box each time you say "true" or agree that you do indeed have the specified quality in yourself. Check in with yourself at each statement and make sure you're answering honestly.

○ I have a lot of energy.

○ I'm a strong person.

○ I hate to be tied down.

○ I always know what to say.

○ I'm great at fixing things.

○ People come to me for advice.

○ I've been called "the life of the party."

○ I tend to suppress my emotions.

○ Other people feel safe with me.

○ I have strong opinions.

○ I'm very protective of those I love.

○ I'm very empathetic toward others.

○ I avoid talking about my deep emotions.

○ I like to help others become the best versions of themselves.

○ I'm good at math and science.

○ I love to travel and see new things.

○ I'm a good public speaker.

○ I get bored easily.

○ I know I have a lot of inner wisdom.

○ I can't stand whining.

○ I tend to psychically know things.

○ I have a small group of close friends and lots of acquaintances.

○ I'm great at telling stories.

○ I'm very expressive.

○ I love to learn.

Checklist A Total:

_____

CHECKLIST B

Read each of the following statements. Check the box each time you say "true" or agree that you do indeed have the specified quality in yourself. Check in with yourself at each statement and make sure you're answering honestly.

○ I'm fiercely independent.

○ My self-confidence is through the roof.

○ I'm a natural-born leader.

○ I have a lot of friends.

○ I tend to be pretty clumsy.

○ I don't necessarily find comfort by looking up into the sky.

○ I know a lot about a lot of different topics.

○ I love food or consider myself a "foodie."

○ I absolutely love cats.

○ People say I'm a trendsetter.

○ I like to influence other people.

○ I'm the definition of an "old soul."

○ I'm very set in my ways.

○ I find other people fascinating.

○ I have a hard time breaking out of bad habits.

○ I feel like I have to save everyone around me.

○ I'm very stubborn.

○ I'm great at trivia.

○ I have catlike features.

○ It feels fun to be a human being.

○ Sometimes it's hard to break out of my comfort zone.

○ I have a hard time committing to other people.

○ I love to "people watch."

○ You could call me a bold person.

○ I'm pretty resilient.

Checklist B Total:

_____

CHECKLIST C

Read each of the following statements. Check the box each time you say "true" or agree that you do indeed have the specified quality in yourself. Check in with yourself at each statement and make sure you're answering honestly.

○ I love to be out in nature.

○ For some reason, animals are drawn to me.

○ I have artistic talents.

○ I care deeply about planet Earth.

○ My imagination is always running wild.

○ I tend to prioritize others' needs before my own.

○ I have a strong sense of intuition.

○ Lying on the Earth's surface relaxes me.

○ I will do anything to avoid conflict.

○ I'm pretty oblivious to how others see me.

○ I consider myself eco-conscious.

○ I want to fix other people.

○ I spend a lot of time daydreaming.

○ Other people's emotions affect me harshly.

○ I've been called "childlike" or "angelic."

○ I tend to attract dysfunctional people.

○ I love animals more than the average person.

○ I feel most at home when I'm outside.

○ Sometimes I know things in my gut to be true.

○ I have trouble expressing myself at times.

○ I'll do everything in my power to protect the planet.

○ I'm a bit of an escapist.

○ I'm very drawn to the arts.

○ I see the good in people.

○ I have a lot of pets.

Checklist C Total:

———————————————

CHECKLIST D

Read each of the following statements. Check the box each time you say "true" or agree that you do indeed have the specified quality in yourself. Check in with yourself at each statement and make sure you're answering honestly.

○ I love to travel all over the world.

○ I have a strong sense of empathy for others.

○ I believe everyone should be treated fairly.

○ I may look like I'm keeping it together but inside I'm a mess.

○ I've been known to break the speed limit.

○ I tend to keep my emotions to myself.

○ I believe the system is broken and needs rebuilding.

○ I love my freedom and will fiercely defend it.

○ I have self-confidence issues.

○ I don't understand why we have to pay taxes.

○ I have a rebellious side.

○ Other people are constantly judging me.

○ I want to help others become the best versions of themselves.

○ I've thought about moving "off the grid" before.

○ Too much structure can be suffocating.

○ I set boundaries with others so they can't hurt me.

○ I can read people like a book.

○ People come to me for advice.

○ I've been called a free spirit.

○ I can't stand overbearing people.

○ I'm really critical of myself.

○ Sometimes I can't help being late.

○ I love to fly on airplanes.

○ I can't sit still.

○ I can't stand liars.

Checklist D Total:

_____

CHECKLIST E

Read each of the following statements. Check the box each time you say "true" or agree that you do indeed have the specified quality in yourself. Check in with yourself at each statement and make sure you're answering honestly.

○ I love to learn.

○ I ask a lot of questions.

○ I'm competitive.

○ I'm quite powerful.

○ I'm very intelligent.

○ I keep my emotions pushed down inside.

○ I'm logically minded.

○ I'm happier alone than in big groups.

○ You could call me "type A."

○ I do my best work on my own.

○ I can be intimidating.

○ I'm not overly emotional.

○ I'm analytical in nature.

○ I tend to overanalyze things.

○ I need validation from others.

○ I've been accused of being too critical.

○ I'm frustrated by people who don't like to learn new things.

○ I'm pretty sensitive.

○ I've been called a "know-it-all."

○ I have a low tolerance for bad teachers.

○ I'm not a social butterfly.

○ I have to be the best.

○ I'm very bright.

○ I'm usually pretty calm.

○ I'm great at trivia.

Checklist E Total:

_____

CHECKLIST F

Read each of the following statements. Check the box each time you say "true" or agree that you do indeed have the specified quality in yourself. Check in with yourself at each statement and make sure you're answering honestly.

- ○ I keep my guard up when it comes to other people.

- ○ I'm a highly spiritual person.

- ○ I don't keep up with fads or trends.

- ○ I've been known to spend much of my time daydreaming.

- ○ It takes time for me to let a new person in.

- ○ I love fantasy books, movies, and shows.

- ○ I've been told I'm "too serious."

- ○ I made sure I live by a body of water.

- ○ I'm slow to open up to new people.

- ○ I take what people say about me very seriously.

- ○ People come to me for advice.

- ○ I'm a dependable and reliable friend.

○ I have a strong moral compass.

○ I have a lot of water signs in my astrological chart.

○ I'm constantly disappointed in other people.

○ I'm a pretty emotional person.

○ I take life as it comes.

○ I've been told I'm an old soul.

○ I have an affinity for dolphins.

○ I don't like to play games with other people.

○ Some have suggested I may have ADHD.

○ I keep my feelings hidden inside.

○ Being around water relaxes me.

○ I'm usually pretty quiet.

○ I'm secretly hilarious.

Checklist F Total:

_____

RESULTS

Carry your totals into the blanks here and star the checklist with the most checked boxes:

Checklist A total: _____

Checklist B total: _____

Checklist C total: _____

Checklist D total: _____

Checklist E total: _____

Checklist F total: _____

If you had the most checks in **Checklist A**, you are most likely an **Arcturian** starseed. Chapter 11 will tell you more about this star lineage.

If you had the most checks in **Checklist B**, you are most likely a **Lyran** starseed. Chapter 9 will tell you more about this star lineage.

If you had the most checks in **Checklist C**, you are most likely a **Pleiadian** starseed. Chapter 6 will tell you more about this star lineage.

If you had the most checks in **Checklist D**, you are most likely an **Andromedan** starseed. Chapter 8 will tell you more about this star lineage.

If you had the most checks in **Checklist E**, you are most likely an **Orion** starseed. Chapter 10 will tell you more about this star lineage.

If you had the most checks in **Checklist F**, you are most likely a **Sirian** starseed. Chapter 7 will tell you more about this star lineage.

Again, be sure to read all of the chapters, not just the ones relating to where you have a high number of checkmarks, because you might find you have influences from more than one star lineage.

Chapter 6
Pleiadians

Now that we've discussed what a starseed is, why they come to Earth, and overviewed the universe as it pertains to them, it's time to start learning about some of the different star lineages. First up are the Pleiadians, a heart-focused race of human-looking star beings from the Pleiadian star system. They are some of the more recent arrivals in the universe compared to Earth and some of the other planets we'll be discussing. They are a loving people who focus much of their energy on bettering the planet Earth and human beings as a whole.

WHAT WE KNOW ABOUT PLEIADIANS

Pleiadians live in the Pleiades star cluster, a group of stars within the constellation Taurus approximately about 400 light-years from Earth. Some people believe Pleiadians originated on a planet called Erra approximately 500 light-years away. Within the Pleiades star system lie over a thousand stars. The brightest of them all is Alcyone, which astronomers have suggested is about seven times as bright as the Sun. This particular star system is believed to be approximately 150 million years old, which is considered fairly young in astronomical terms. As such, Pleiadians are seen as some of the younger souls of the star system. (For context, Earth is approximately 4.5 billion years old.)

Pleiadians have been reported to travel in stereotypical spaceships, though they are also able to travel freely through space-time (or time travel, if you will). It's also believed Pleiadians can move between the third and ninth dimensions with ease.

Where They're From

In astronomy, the Pleiades star grouping is also referred to as the Seven Sisters. Since these stars can easily be seen by the human eye, we know they are extremely bright. If you look at the cluster with a powerful enough telescope, you can make out over one thousand component stars. With the human eye alone we can see six or seven of them from almost any vantage point on Earth. The brightness of six of the stars actually changes throughout the course of a day while the seventh star's brightness fluctuates over the course of one or two weeks, thus making it so only six stars are usually visible in the cluster at any one time. To find the group easily in the night sky, draw a line from Orion's Belt to his bow and continue following that line until you reach the Taurus constellation.

The Greek Story of the Pleiades

For more on the Seven Sisters and the Pleiades, we can turn to Greek mythology. According to ancient myth, the Pleiades were the seven daughters of Atlas. Their names were Maia, Electra, Alcyone, Taygete, Asterope, Celaeno, and Merope. These "heavenly sisters" each bore children with Olympian gods, such as Zeus, Poseidon, Ares, and Orion. The legend goes that, when Atlas fought alongside the Titans against Zeus and lost, Zeus sentenced him to hold up the celestial heavens for all eternity as punishment. Atlas's daughters, the seven sisters, were so despondent over the fate of their father that Zeus took pity on them and allowed them to live among the stars so they could be close to Atlas.

The Native American Story of the Pleiades

Native Americans have many allegories about this particular star system. Many tribes consider the Pleiades to be a sacred place in the heavens. For example:

- Lakota folklore states that humans originated from the Pleiades and will return to it once they've lived their lives on Earth. They believe our job as humans on this planet is to care for and protect the Earth.

- The Nez Perce tribe has a similar folklore surrounding the Pleiades to that in Greek mythology but with a different spin. Within the group of seven sisters, one of the sisters falls in love with a human man whose eventual death destroys her. Her six sisters make fun of how sad she is over his death, so she keeps her sadness bottled up deep inside until it completely consumes her. She then pulls the sky over her face so she can't be seen, thus explaining why the seventh sister (or star) often can't be seen.

- The Kiowa nation's folklore suggests that seven little girls were chased by bears onto a low rock. They prayed for the rock to save them from the bears, and the rock suddenly grew higher and higher into the sky until the girls eventually rested, becoming the Pleiades. The rock that grew to such great heights is believed to be Devils Tower in Wyoming, which has long grooves along its sides said to be claw marks from the bears pursuing the girls.

- The Cherokee have a different origin story for how the Pleiades star system was first formed. As the legend goes, seven young boys spent so much time playing a game with a stone wheel that their mothers decided to teach them a lesson by serving them boiled rocks for dinner. The boys were so angered by their treatment that they decided to go someplace where they wouldn't be a bother to their mothers. They prayed for spirits to guide them and began to dance. As they danced, they rose higher and higher into the sky until their mothers saw them and tried to pull them back down. One mother was successful in pulling her son down but she did it with such force that she pulled him into the ground, causing the earth to collapse around them. The other six boys rose up into the sky to form the stars we now see as the Pleiades. This is why the Cherokee refer to the star group as Ani'tsutsa, which translates into English as "the boys."

What They Look Like

Most Pleiadians have a "Nordic-like" appearance: light-colored eyes, light or blonde hair, and fair or lightly tanned skin. They tend to have well-defined jawlines or cheekbones on their long faces and are usually very tall, averaging between six and seven feet in height. They're said to radiate a glowing, beautiful energy that adds to their angelic appearance. This luminosity is probably why they are often mistaken for angels when visiting or seen by humans.

Their Purpose on Earth

Pleiadians are all about the energetic heart center or heart chakra. They go around bringing about peace and sharing their wisdom. They want to help humans achieve their heart-centered nature. To do so, people must spend time working on themselves and healing their heart centers. Pleiadians want you to embrace who you are—mind, body, and soul—for all the beauty and exquisiteness they behold. When you heal yourself and radiate your heart energy at its highest frequency, you're actually sharing this vibration with everyone you come into contact with. You don't have to do anything to share this joyous vibration other than to live happily and keep working on yourself.

Pleiadians are all about the energetic heart center or heart chakra.

It could be the similarities between humans and Pleiadians that lead Pleiadians to want to help heal and transform humans into high-frequency, radiant beings. It's said the Pleiadian realm is the next step in human evolution. Pleiadians are often believed to be sending and channeling messages to us so we can gain knowledge we wouldn't have otherwise. They bring their wisdom to us via these nonthreatening methods to help Earth ascend to the next level.

Barbara Marciniak's Pleiadian Messages

The most well-known human to have channeled messages from the Pleiadians is Barbara Marciniak, who has been receiving messages since May of 1988. She's written many books, releases a quarterly newsletter called *The Pleiadian Times*, and shares information through her *YouTube* page.

TRAITS OF PLEIADIAN STARSEEDS

So, how do starseeds with a Pleiadian background act on Earth during their human lifetimes? While no Pleiadian starseeds are exactly the same, of course, they do share some common traits, all of which hold true for non-starseed Pleiadians as well. In general, they are extremely talented and gifted people who use their many skills to better the lives of others on Earth. Let's look at some of their qualities.

They Love the Earth

Pleiadian starseeds have an intense love for planet Earth. They have a specific drive to protect it by any means necessary, perhaps more so than any other star lineages. Considering Pleiadians have a mission to help humans and our planet, it makes sense that Pleiadian starseeds would inherit the same traits. These starseeds:

- Tend to be very eco-conscious and try not to buy wasteful material objects.

- Reuse everything they can.

- Speak out about the horrible way capitalistic society treats the sacred ground we all live on and cannot stand the decimation of natural lands.

- Truly appreciate the beauty our planet has and will do anything they can to protect it.

- Love nature. Pleiadian starseeds love to spend time outdoors in any natural environment, from rocky mountains to sunny beaches. They can be adventurer types who enjoy going on hikes or participating in more extreme outdoor sports. When they want to relax, they spend time outdoors to help calm themselves. Lying down in the grass, lying on the beach, or even just smelling fresh air can cause them to instantly forget their woes. These types of starseeds can be partial to "earthing" (the habit of walking or standing barefoot outdoors). Whether they are doing it for this purpose or not, earthing allows you to absorb the Earth's grounding energy through your feet and send your undesired energy into the ground.

They Love Animals

Pleiadian starseeds have a strong affinity for animals. Animals like to be around them and they love to be near animals. These starseeds have a special knack for training animals and may have a lot of pets in their home. They might also be a "magnet" for the neighborhood's pets and wild animals, who are drawn to their specific energy. They can easily become veterinarians or biologists, or pursue other vocations that involve working with living creatures.

They Have a Strong Connection with the Heart

Pleiadian starseeds are magnetic, charming people who don't always necessarily know they come off this way. In fact, they can be totally oblivious to how others perceive them. These starseeds have extremely strong heart chakras that, once activated, can be intensely powerful. As with the Pleiadian star beings, these starseeds have a strong desire to heal others. When operating with a high frequency and a healthy heart chakra, they can tell when other people's chakras are out of sync and will want to do anything they can to assist in sorting that out.

They Can Have Weak Throat Chakras

Pleiadian starseeds are also known to have weak throat chakras. The throat chakra (the fifth chakra, called *Visuddha* in Sanskrit) is the center for expression and communication. When it's out of sync, you're unable to speak your truth and prioritize others' needs before your own. This is especially true for starseeds, who have an innate yearning to help people.

Being unable to prioritize your own needs can become a problem because Pleiadian starseeds tend to attract dysfunctional people into their lives. It usually occurs because of their desire to "fix" other people combined with putting others' needs before their own and their inability to advocate for themselves. This is why they tend to get taken advantage of and hurt repeatedly by those they've given their affection and attention to.

If you see these traits in yourself, it's not too late to work on them! You can spend time focusing on your throat chakra and creating healthy boundaries to keep from being easily hurt by others.

Pleiadian Starseed, Heal Thyself

Pleiadian starseeds with heart chakras that are not activated or are out of balance can have major self-worth issues. They don't see what others see in them and are extremely hard on themselves. They are often oblivious to the praise given by others or refuse to accept it.

They're In Tune with Their Intuition

Starseeds of Pleiadian descent are extremely in tune with their intuition. It helps guide them throughout their lives on Earth and allows them to pick up on signals that aren't available to those not in tune with this frequency. They often know things in their gut they couldn't know otherwise or can tell when something isn't quite right. Sometimes this manifests as the psychic skills discussed earlier in the book, like clairvoyance or telepathy. They're able to take a more holistic view of the world and their lives and not be so caught up in the everyday dramas of human life. They're also able to regularly pick up on synchronicities throughout their day.

However, this strong sense of intuition also means they pick up on other people's emotions in a vivid way and can be highly affected by them. Pleiadians tend to empathically feel other people's emotions and thus must carefully choose who they let into their lives. Without erecting boundaries to protect themselves, their mood can swing based on who's around them.

Pleiadians tend to empathically feel other people's emotions and thus must carefully choose who they let into their lives.

They Like to Daydream

Pleiadian starseeds are dreamy, idealistic people who are drawn to escapism. Their eyes often glaze over as their imagination runs wild and they daydream the day away. Sometimes they actually prefer to be in these dreamlike states rather than live in the reality of everyday life. They can be childlike in this way, which ultimately ties in to their pure heart and soul. They have a hard time comprehending the darkness they see in the world and would prefer not to engage in it. In fact, they have a really hard time with conflict and will do anything in their power to avoid it. They'd rather let an issue fester and avoid speaking about it out loud rather than confront or be confronted by another person. When conflict does arise, they tend to retreat immediately or say whatever they can to end the dispute as quickly as possible.

They Are Drawn to the Arts

Pleiadian starseeds are also natural healers who are drawn to the arts. They're often strongly connected to lightwork and healing modalities due to their intense desire to heal others. They've been known to excel at creative arts like sculpting, painting, singing, playing instruments, and dancing, among others. In fact, starseeds of Pleiadian descent are especially adept at using the arts to help heal people.

Chapter 7
Sirians

Next up on our tour of the different star lineages of the universe are Sirians. These highly intelligent beings live on the predominantly water-based star Sirius. It is well known among ancient cultures because it also happens to be the brightest star in Earth's sky. These star beings have a mission to help humanity ascend to the next level and consider themselves to be our protectors and guardians. They're also skilled alchemists with a lot of personal integrity.

WHAT WE KNOW ABOUT SIRIANS

Sirians live on Sirius, widely known as the brightest star in Earth's sky. Scientists estimate it is twenty-five times brighter than our Sun and twice its size. In fact, it is slowly inching closer to our solar system, so it will become even brighter over the next 60,000 years. The name Sirius comes from the Greek word *seirios*, which translates to "scorching" or "glowing" and speaks to how bright it is in our sky. It sits about 8.6 light-years away from Earth, making it the fifth closest star system we know of.

Where They're From

Sirius is sometimes referred to as the "Dog Star" because it's the most prominent star in the Canis Major constellation (Latin for "the greater dog"). Have you ever heard the expression "the dog days of summer"? Well, that phrase comes from a specific time during the summer months in the Northern Hemisphere when Sirius can be seen rising in conjunction with the Sun. You can check out this phenomenon for yourself between the dates of July 3 and August 11. Based on its position relative to the constellation Orion, some cultures also thought Sirius was doglike because it's located where a dog would walk next to its owner. In *The Iliad*, Homer even refers to Sirius as "Orion's dog."

To find Sirius in the night sky, you can use Orion as your guide. Focus on the three stars that make up Orion's Belt—Alnilam, Alnitak, and Mintaka—then follow the belt downward to the left about eight times the length of the three stars and you'll find Sirius. Given how bright it is, it's hard to miss, but it does appear brightest between January and March.

Sirius A and Sirius B

When we look up at the stars and see this brightly glowing spot in the sky, we're actually seeing Sirius A, one of two companion stars that circle each other. Sirius B was discovered in 1862 by astronomers who were completely surprised by the revelation because Sirius A was so well known and easily visible with the human eye. Sirius A and Sirius B slowly revolve around each other in a cycle that completes every fifty years. Believed to be the same size as the Sun, Sirius B is a white dwarf star that is only a fraction the size of Sirius A. Scientists believe it was a much bigger, full-sized star for millions of years but has since collapsed into a small, weakened version of what it once was. (Throughout this chapter, we will simply refer to Sirius A as Sirius and note whenever a reference is instead to Sirius B.)

The color of Sirius in our night sky is a bluish white that can sometimes be seen flickering into a rainbow of other colors. This color-changing trait is one all stars share, but because Sirius is so bright in our night sky, it makes it easier to observe this phenomenon.

The Ancient Egyptian Connection to Sirius

Sirius was highly important to the ancient Egyptians, who put great effort toward tracking and recording changes in the night sky. They noticed Sirius rose right before the Sun, called a heliacal rising, every year the Nile river flooded. This rising of the river was monumental in their world as it would devastate some of their land but also nourish and feed their crops. It's believed they based their calendar on this event and Sirius's position in the sky. Many ancient Egyptian gods and goddesses have strong ties to Sirius, such as Sopdet, Osiris, Isis, and Hathor. It's believed many of the pyramids in Egypt are aligned with certain stars, and the Great Pyramid of Giza is supposedly in perfect alignment with Sirius.

Sirius and Polynesian Navigation

Polynesian cultures also found Sirius to be important. It's believed they based their navigation system for sailing around the Pacific Ocean on this star system. It's part of the great bird constellation called Manu that divides the sky into the Southern and Northern Hemispheres and was used to track the location of other points in the night sky.

What Do They Look Like?

Sirians come from a very diverse world believed to be made mostly of water. It's said dolphins, mermaids, whales, and other sea creatures can roam freely there. The people of Sirius are said to be a wide array of high-dimensional beings, such as lion people, bird people, merpeople, aquatic beings, feline beings, and humanoids that look similar to humans on Earth. Such a large variety of beings on Sirius means they vary greatly in nature and appearance.

Their Purpose on Earth

Sirians are highly ascended beings who are guardians and protectors of Earth. They treat humans with love, kindness, and respect. They want to see us ascend to a higher state of consciousness in order to become their equals. They do what they can to help us move from being animals to being spiritual beings and from being carbon-based life-forms to being crystalline life-forms. They're known to be incredible alchemists, teachers, and masters of science.

Sirians are highly
ascended beings who
are guardians and
protectors of Earth.

Traveling via Interdimensional Pathway

It's said Sirians are able to travel throughout the universe and that they've built an interdimensional pathway to visit us on Earth. Many believe they've been guiding humanity throughout history by sharing their teachings with humans. Some believe they helped build the pyramids, assisted in the creation of what we call witchcraft, and helped ancient lost cities like Atlantis flourish.

TRAITS OF SIRIAN STARSEEDS

Sirians share many of the general characteristics of starseeds but have some unique qualities as well.

They Want to Understand Humans

Sirians want to use their human lifetimes on our planet to truly understand human beings. They're here to learn the struggles of being a person on Earth and learn why we are the way we are. How can they help us properly if they don't really understand us? Once a Sirian starseed awakens to their mission, they enter into a state of service for the planet and its people lasting the rest of their human lifetime. They will often act as guides or teachers for those who are struggling spiritually or otherwise need assistance.

They Love the Water

Sirian starseeds have a major affinity for the water—living by it, swimming in it, drinking it, you name it. This stems from their home-world being a planet made of water. Being near water is soothing, comforting, and even vaguely nostalgic to them. You'll find many Sirian starseeds living next to lakes, rivers, oceans, streams, or any other body of water. They'll often have flowing water in their house, via fountains or fish tanks, and are known to take long showers or indulgent baths. They're also drawn to the energy of dolphins and the vibrations of the ocean.

They find water to be particularly cleansing for their energy, helping to reset their emotions and feelings from the day. Those who ascribe to astrology have noted that many Sirian starseeds have a lot of water signs throughout their chart.

They Are a Calming Influence on People

Just as all forms of water are calming to Sirian starseeds and help them release their pent-up energy, Sirian starseeds tend to have that same effect on other people. Others are drawn to their energy and will often come to them for advice. As those seeking advice voice their problems, they feel comforted just by speaking with the starseed. It's said the eyes of Sirian starseeds have an extreme emotional depth and that you can understand things just by looking into them. Sirian starseeds tend to be perceived as being quite serious, so there is also a feeling of authority both within them and that is understood by others.

They Feel Emotions Deeply

Sirian starseeds feel their emotions rather deeply. They may be able to hide their feelings quite well at times, but underneath the surface, there's usually a lot more to the story. Sirians take the words others say about them to heart. They're easily stung by the biting words of others and tend to internalize them for a long time.

They keep their guard high, so it's usually quite difficult to penetrate it and become their friend. While they can be a great shoulder to cry on, they tend to have a hard time expressing their own feelings to others. In fact, they even have a hard time expressing their feelings to themselves. They tend to need time to reflect on how they're feeling in order to process it.

This is something to note about your Sirian starseed friends or partners—they usually require time to process and understand their emotions before they can truly speak on them. It's best to allow them the time they need and encourage communication as much as you can. Be there when they do decide to open up to you and, whatever you do, don't judge them.

They Have Quiet Personalities

Starseeds of Sirian descent tend to be pretty quiet in nature. This can mean they're slow to open up to new people and don't spend a lot of their time attempting to make friends. They can appear as loners, though they don't see anything wrong with mostly keeping to themselves. They prefer to spend their time learning about things that interest them or engaging in fascinating pursuits rather than partying, drinking, or fooling around.

They don't really follow trends or care about what's deemed to be popular. While they may choose to ascribe to a certain lifestyle (think goth, hippie, punk, and so on), they can't be defined by this. They are truly unique, and, even when they do choose to categorize themselves or participate in these subgroups, they are still totally unique within those confines. They can't help but express themselves in their own unique ways.

They Have a Lot of Integrity

Sirian starseeds tend to have intense integrity and extremely high morals, to the point where they are often let down by those around them. They will eventually learn how to forgive others for what they say or to take measures to avoid being hurt again. Because of this, they don't actively try to recruit new pals or allow themselves to be trampled by other people. Sirians tend to keep a small circle of trusted people in their lives. When they do make friends, they are extremely devoted and dependable and will do everything they can to honor those friendships, at least until they're disappointed. If that happens, they will often move on. If you disappoint a Sirian starseed, it is very difficult to make it back into their good graces because they don't want to be hurt again.

Sirians tend to keep a small circle of trusted people in their lives.

They treat others how they want to be treated and are often called "old souls." Some even suggest they radiate a frequency of "seriousness," which can be intimidating to some, especially those who haven't taken the time to work on themselves.

They Love the Fantasy Genre

Another shared characteristic of Sirian starseeds is their love of fantasy. This could mean they're obsessed with movies, books, or TV shows set in that genre. This type of entertainment reminds them of the wild and fantastical world they once lived in on Sirius. They also appreciate that many fantasy-themed writings and series tend to mention supposedly imaginary beings—such as merpeople, fairies, and leprechauns—that Sirian starseeds know deep inside do exist elsewhere in the universe (and sometimes even on Earth).

They Are Spiritual Beings

Sirian starseeds are often highly spiritual beings. Because of their connection to Sirius, they are innately attuned or "hardwired" to a higher frequency that allows their consciousness to expand faster than the average human. As a result, they tend to be spiritual people who develop their own spiritual practices and routines. They are very intelligent and seek out information about their spiritual studies across the globe. Their studies and learnings generally result in a calm, relaxed presence that can handle pretty much whatever life throws their way.

If a Sirian starseed hasn't started to explore their spirituality yet, it usually means they're actively blocking it for some reason, perhaps due to trauma or shaming. If you're reading this and can relate, it's time to let the walls down and start tuning into your inner self, unlocking many lessons for you to learn.

They Have a Lively Imagination

Sirian starseeds have a wild imagination and are known to get lost in it quite often. From their perspective, it's much more fun and entertaining to spend time in their own mind than to be experiencing our three-dimensional lives. Some Sirian starseeds may have been given the label of ADD or ADHD when they were children or young adults. One reason they might have trouble paying attention is they simply aren't satisfied with what they see and experience here on Earth. They'd much rather be swimming with dolphins or traveling to different worlds than sitting in a classroom or bored at a desk job.

They Are Unique

Sirian starseeds express themselves fully, both in the words they say and how they present themselves. They usually have a unique look about them and enjoy not following current trends. Some of them love to wear wild clothing to make a statement while others prefer to blend in and wear the same not-so-exciting duds every day.

They Have a Great Sense of Humor

When it comes to expressing their words, Sirian starseeds' knack for humor can't be beat. They always come up with a great punchline to any story or joke. They can be really silly in nature and they always provide a laugh when someone needs one. Usually they'll only be humorous with those they fully trust, so when you befriend a Sirian starseed you should be prepared to laugh. They are also great storytellers.

They Are Great Healers

Starseeds with Sirian lineage also make great healers. They often become lightworkers, shamans, and other types of healing professionals. Once they've healed themselves, they feel it's their duty to help others do the same. They love taking others under their wing and teaching them all they know about spirituality. They've been known to be interested in crystals, tarot cards, astrology, and other supposedly "occult" tools and subjects. They're very open to different aspects of spirituality and love to learn new things.

Chapter 8
Andromedans

Unlike Pleiadians and Sirians, Andromedan starseeds come from a galaxy far, far away— millions of light-years, in fact! Andromedans are a highly intelligent species that live on a planet encompassing a wide variety of beings. They want to shake things up on Earth and help us usher in a new world. Andromedan starseeds are rebellious people who fight for their own freedom, love to travel, and live by their own rules. While they struggle with self-criticism, they are widely loved and respected and have arrived on this planet to help others heal.

WHAT WE KNOW ABOUT ANDROMEDANS

Andromedan star beings come from the spiral-shaped Andromeda Galaxy, the largest galaxy in our local galactic cluster and the closest to our own. It's estimated to be about twice as large across as the Milky Way and to contain more than a trillion stars, as many as four times the number in our home galaxy.

Scientists believe there are at least twenty-five dwarf galaxies within the Andromeda Galaxy as well. These smaller, satellite galaxies revolve around an inner core that contains a black hole, just as in our own galaxy. While Andromeda is currently more than 2.5 million light-years away from the Milky Way, the two galaxies are on a collision course. However, scientists don't believe it will be some big crash. It's more likely it will be akin to two galaxies getting scrambled around a bit and settling into new positions. Don't worry, though: This isn't expected to happen for another four billion years!

Where They Come From

The Andromeda Galaxy can be seen by the human eye from Earth and is the most distant celestial object that can be seen without any technological assistance. To find the V-shaped Andromeda constellation in Earth's night sky, look between Cassiopeia and the Great Square within the Pegasus constellation.

If you can identify the Milky Way, Andromeda can be found by looking just underneath the protrusion of its lower middle part. In the Northern Hemisphere, Andromeda is most clearly viewed in the fall, while in the Southern Hemisphere it can be seen between October and December.

Hubble's Discovery

Centuries ago, Andromeda was believed to be some kind of nebular object out in space. However, in 1923, astronomer Edwin Hubble was able to distinguish a Cepheid variable star within the Andromeda Galaxy. By spotting this, he was able to discern that if you know how bright something is, you can calculate the distance between you and that object. This was a huge moment in history that forever changed the way humans looked at space. We had no reason to believe we weren't the only galaxy in the universe before this discovery. Once Andromeda was identified as a galaxy, it opened up endless possibilities in the night sky.

The Greek Story of Andromeda

In Greek mythology, Andromeda was a princess born to Cassiopeia and King Cepheus of Ethiopia. Legend states that her parents bragged to Poseidon that their daughter was prettier than the famously gorgeous sea nymphs. Poseidon sent a sea monster to the parents and suggested they sacrifice their daughter to save the rest of the country. Her father relented, chaining Andromeda to a rock and leaving her as a sacrifice. Upon discovering this, Perseus offered to save her from the sea monster under the condition that he be allowed to marry her if successful. He did save her, and the two eventually wed, became king and queen of Mycenae and Tiryns, and had seven children. Upon Andromeda's death, the goddess Athena sent her to rest among the stars in what became the Andromeda constellation.

Their Purpose on Earth

The Greek name Andromeda translates into English as "ruler of men." Andromedans spend a lot of their time protecting and teaching us. Andromedans are known as the holders of great wisdom. They're believed to be immortal seers, healers, and masters of time. They want to help usher in the Age of Aquarius and bring an ascended knowledge to the masses. Andromedans also spend time trying to aid humanity by renewing the planet across all categories—our governments, our environment, and the way we treat ourselves and each other. Their teachings are about time being limitless (or an illusion), and they share comforting messages about embracing death, explaining that we are all energy that cannot disappear. They exist between the third and twelfth dimensions.

Andromedans are
known as the holders
of great wisdom.

What They Look Like

Unlike some star lineages, Andromedans do not have stereotypical physical traits that are all the same. Andromeda is filled with many different types of beings who can choose to look any way they'd like:

- Their skin can be any color of the rainbow.

- Andromedans can be short or tall. Some are elegant, some are angelic, and some are elven-looking.

- They can have wings.

- They can have cone-shaped heads and wide eyes.

- Some have been said to appear as humanlike people wearing all white.

- Others have said they appear as light beings without any physical characteristics.

Being masters of the metaphysical, it's likely they choose how they want to appear to others whenever they make contact with another being. It's believed they can choose to exist in a material state of being or as a bright light.

TRAITS OF ANDROMEDAN STARSEEDS

Just as there are many different types of Andromedan personalities, there are just as many traits that can come through during a starseed's lifetime on Earth. Following are some common qualities.

They Are Free Spirits

Andromedan starseeds are the definition of free spirits. They get bored easily and don't like to be confined, whether physically (at home, in jail, etc.) or metaphorically (feeling trapped). This can manifest in a number of different ways, one being the inability to be "tied down." They will often have issues sticking to the same job, relationship, hometown, or any other sort of commitment. It's really difficult for these types of starseeds to make big decisions in life, such as choosing to get married, accepting a job, or moving to a new place. It can be equally hard for them to figure out smaller, everyday decisions, like what to eat, what to wear, or what to read. You could definitely call them commitment-phobes.

They Love to Travel

Starseeds of the Andromedan lineage are known to love traveling—and traveling at great speeds. They seem to constantly be in motion. On a local level, this might look like someone who is constantly taking scenic drives, bike rides, or walks through the neighborhood. On a bigger scale, many of these types will travel great distances within their own state or country, or they may become world travelers. It's safe to say Andromedan starseeds have the "travel bug" and, if they can afford to do so, will go on lots of vacations to far-off places.

They also love to go fast when they travel! This means they like to speed when they're in the car or use boats, jet skis, and other fast vehicles, and they absolutely love to fly on airplanes. It's believed the connection here is that the fast movement and air travel reminds Andromedan starseeds of how they would travel at home on Andromeda.

They Love Freedom

Andromedan starseeds are lovers of freedom and will do anything to protect their own. They have an innate thirst for it and do not like to be told what to do. They want to break out of the system and ignite others to do the same. These starseeds especially do not like structure. This even applies to the idea of time itself, so they are known to consistently be late.

Looking at the bigger picture, they'd like to tear down society as it is now and build brand-new ways of living going forward. This often translates to a distaste toward government or other people in power. They don't like having to pay taxes, and they get frustrated if they don't feel like they have enough of a say on how collected taxes are allocated. They have a hard time grasping the concept of having to pay to live on the planet on which they were born.

Andromedan starseeds have almost definitely spent time fantasizing about "going off-grid" or living alone out in nature. They're the type to learn how to grow their own food and become self-sustainable. They could even be wanderers or nomads who don't identify as having a home base. Some are complete rebels who can be tempted by anarchy (but they usually restrain themselves from going too far). As children, they can feel stifled by overbearing parents.

Of course, the more extreme measures aren't present in every starseed of Andromedan lineage, but the love and defense of their freedom will exist inside them regardless of how or if it manifests. Some may seek it their entire lives while others will learn the lessons necessary to grow out of it. Mature starseeds will eventually learn to stop running and seeking out freedom however they can because they'll understand it's not the specifics of their own circumstances that will fulfill this need. They'll have to learn to feel freedom within themselves through working on their inner selves and establishing a true sense of self-love.

They Are Highly Empathetic

Andromedan starseeds are highly empathetic and compassionate people. They are extremely sensitive to what's going on with the masses and can likewise pinpoint when something is wrong with almost any individual. They can see through emotional manipulation easily and refuse to put up with it.

Andromedan starseeds
are highly empathetic
and compassionate
people.

They Value Truth and Fairness

They have a low tolerance for lies and people who lie often. They appreciate those who speak the truth and mean what they say. They can't stand being treated unfairly and do not tolerate seeing others dealing with injustice. They believe all humans should be treated equally and with fairness—and are consistently heartbroken when society does otherwise.

They Love to Empower Others

In their work, Andromedan starseeds tend to gravitate toward professions that empower others to become better versions of themselves. They like to help people gain control of their lives. They have a strong desire to work on healing humankind's emotional, physical, and psychic pain and can be drawn to healing modalities such as Reiki, acupuncture, yoga, massage, and other holistic pursuits.

Many people of this starseed lineage are able to uplift others with very little effort. This happens through healing, yes, but also with giving good advice—something Andromedan starseeds are great at. In fact, their solid advice is sought out by their friends, relatives, and loved ones all the time—and sometimes even random strangers will approach them for some words of wisdom. They should take it as a compliment!

Their Personalities Run the Gamut

Some Andromedan starseeds are extremely punk rock about the way they live—they're really "in your face" with their ideas and often dress eccentrically. These personalities want to draw attention to themselves and the way they are to help shake things up in the world. They also want to increase acceptance of those who aren't like everyone else.

Meanwhile, other Andromedan starseeds are much more laid-back. They have a very soft yet expressive energy and usually blend in with the rest of society. These types tend to become teachers and healers in their lifetimes on Earth.

They Can Be Too Self-Critical

Not all Andromedan starseeds are perfect energetic beings who are totally and completely enlightened. It takes time and effort to achieve that level of spiritual enlightenment (and some never actually do). Most of them struggle with being too self-critical. They put up emotional boundaries and refuse to let untrusted people in. They often don't take themselves seriously and can't comprehend how truly amazing they are.

Their constant self-criticism can also cause them to expect that others are looking at them with the same critical eye. In fact, they're surprised to find out how well liked by other people they actually are. Their lack of self-confidence leads them to feel like they aren't well received generally but nothing could be further from the truth. These starseeds are great at communication and make friends with ease.

You would never pick up on a lack of self-confidence in any Andromedan starseed. They are excellent at keeping their inner fears, insecurities, and self-doubts deep inside where no one can see them. They present a version of themselves that looks completely put together to other people. If this situation resonates with you, you're not alone. While this may seem like a strength to most, it also can be confusing for others—and yourself. For one, if you seem like you're totally fine all the time (even when inside you're not), it will be hard for others to pick up on any problems and ask if you're okay. It also means your peers will consistently believe you can handle pretty much everything. Know that it's okay to show your honest thoughts, feelings, and experiences and that the more honest you can be with others, the more honest you can be with yourself. It's okay to not be okay and to rely on others when you need to.

Chapter 9
Lyrans

Lyrans hail from Lyra, the lyre constellation. These ancient star beings are some of if not the oldest in the galaxy. They spread a message of love and self-acceptance. Lyran starseeds are often confident, enigmatic people who tend to become leaders and inspire others. Their lives on Lyra were often feline in nature, which has led Lyran starseeds to feel clumsy at times in their human bodies. Overall, they are bold and trendy people who can easily become leaders due to the respect they gain from others.

WHAT WE KNOW ABOUT LYRANS

Lyrans originally hail from the ancient constellation Lyra. This grouping of stars represents the lyre, a stringed musical instrument that looks like a mini U-shaped harp. It's closest star, Vega, is just over 25 light-years away, making Lyra one of the closest constellations to Earth. It was first catalogued all the way back in the second century by Greek astronomer Ptolemy and is estimated to be more than 800 million years old.

The constellation is sometimes represented as a vulture or an eagle carrying a lyre and is also called Aquila Cadens ("falling eagle") or Vultur Cadens ("falling vulture"). Vega, the brightest star in the Lyra constellation, gets its name from the Arabic word *waqi*, meaning "falling" or "swooping." Vega is the fifth-brightest star we can see from Earth and the second-brightest star visible in the Northern Hemisphere.

Where They Come From

Lyra is relatively small in size, being the fifty-second largest out of the eighty-eight officially recognized constellations, and it has a number of stars with their own planets. Three different meteor showers are associated with this constellation: the Lyrids, the June Lyrids, and the Alpha Lyrids.

To find Lyra, start by locating Cygnus, the Swan constellation. Lyra is right next to it and looks like a rhombus. Or you can find Vega, its brightest star, first. Vega is bordered by Draco, Hercules, Vulpecula, and Cygnus. It's best seen in the Northern Hemisphere between June and October.

The Greek Story of Lyra

Greek mythology once again has an origin story for the constellation Lyra. To them, Lyra represented the lyre that belonged to Orpheus. Their stories suggest that Hermes made the first-ever lyre out of a tortoise shell, and Apollo gave it to Orpheus. The music Orpheus played was so beautiful that it brought inanimate objects like trees and rocks to life, so powerful that it was able to silence the song of the Sirens. Rivers would supposedly change direction in order to be closer to it.

Eventually, Orpheus's musical talents charmed a lovely nymph named Eurydice. Shortly after they wed, a snake bit Eurydice and she died. Orpheus traveled to the underworld to rescue her and, through his music, was able to convince Hades to let him bring Eurydice back from the dead under the condition that he would not look back at her until they had left the underworld. Tragically, Orpheus's gaze drifted toward his beloved right before they surfaced and she immediately vanished back into the underworld. Orpheus spent the rest of his days consumed by grief, wandering around Greece until he was eventually murdered. The Muses buried him, and Apollo set his magical lyre into the sky, where Lyra is today.

Other Cultural Associations of Lyra

Other ancient cultures from across the world have different interpretations of the Lyra constellation.

- In Wales, it is referred to as King Arthur's Harp.

- The Persian poet Hafiz called it the Lyre of Zurah.

- The Incas worshipped the same constellation but called it Urcuchillay, who they saw as a llama deity who watched over their animals.

- Australian Aboriginals deemed it to be a birdlike constellation as they named it Malleefowl after the bird species of the same name.

What They Look Like

Lyrans are believed to be the first ancestors of the Pleiadians, and their humanoid-type bodies, like ours, may have originated from their star system. It's suggested they could be the original ancestors of the entire galaxy. Many of them have feline or lionlike features about them: long ears, elvish looks, and large catlike eyes. However, due to their long and complicated galactic history, there are a wide variety of beings that are of Lyran descent. They are an extremely proud star nation of people who have knowledge beyond measure. This characteristic turned brutal when their cultures began to disagree with each other and started a full-on war in outer space. However, much time has passed since then and Lyran cultures have evolved to live in peace, with all existing as one. They inhabit the ninth dimension.

Their Mission on Earth

Like other starseeds, Lyrans are here to help humanity. They're particularly concerned with humans' lack of self-confidence in today's modern world. So many of us have characteristics about which we feel inadequate. We don't think we're smart enough, beautiful enough, funny enough, successful enough, strong enough, or that we even deserve love. The Lyran message is that we are all worthy and deserving of limitless love. They promote body positivity and self-love, believing we are all a significant part of the universe and that we must all gain the confidence we need to shine.

The Lyran message is
that we are all worthy
and deserving of
limitless love.

TRAITS OF LYRAN STARSEEDS

Like all starseeds, Lyrans share some key qualities that help them execute their mission on Earth.

They Are Courageous

Lyran starseeds are very strong and courageous souls. Given that their star lineage is some of the oldest in the galaxy, they relate to being called an "old soul." They have an emotional and intelligent depth that speaks to their age-old wisdom. Lyran starseeds are resilient people, often having chosen a challenging life to lead on the earthly plane. They have a brave, warrior-like energy inside them that is ready to spring into action whenever necessary.

They Can Be Strong-Willed

Lyran starseeds can be extremely stubborn. (Again, that's perhaps thanks to their significant galactic age.) It's not that they're unwilling to try new things, but they definitely prefer to stay in their comfort zones. Their stubbornness also extends to the experiences they've had in their life on Earth. They have a really hard time letting go of their old stories and narratives about society and themselves. Lyran starseeds also hang on to their past wounds and do not try to heal them. They may wear their "battle wounds" like a badge of pride or attach their sob stories to their personality. In order to grow and learn, however, they need to break out of this type of thinking.

Starseeds of Lyran descent have a hard time breaking out of old habits and letting go of stories because they've held on to them for so long. Sometimes their shadow side becomes too comfortable of a place for them to hide. They may be afraid of the spiritual path or the power they believe may be inside them. Or they feel ashamed of it because of how people have shamed or made fun of them in this or previous lifetimes. However, if they want to advance in their spiritual studies and increase their vibration, they'll need to tackle this trauma.

These particular starseeds tend to have issues with their solar plexus chakra (the third chakra, called *Manipura* in Sanskrit). This particular chakra is tied to personal power and is our power source. When starseeds cleanse and energize this power source, they can become the peaceful warriors they truly are inside.

They're Trendsetters

In modern-day society, Lyran starseeds tend to be trendsetters. They will often wear a piece of clothing or discover a book weeks or months before it explodes in popularity. These starseeds are widely beloved people who tend to be, well, popular. They have extremely bold personalities and tend to wear bold clothing, make bold decisions, and be bold with their actions. They don't keep their feelings to themselves and are very confident people. They're known to attract many friends and lovers just by living the way that they do.

They Are Leaders

Lyran starseeds like to "people watch" and analyze social interactions. This interest often inspires them to take on leadership roles, whether it be a job in local government or as the CEO of a business. They might take on smaller leadership roles, too, like leading a book club or being the one person in a group project who does all the work. Lyrans tend to have really big ideas and enjoy trying to make them come to life. They don't mind being in charge, and they love being influential to other people. On the other hand, this can sometimes translate into a savior complex or the feeling that they're bearing the weight of the world on their shoulders.

Lyrans tend to have really big ideas and enjoy trying to make them come to life.

They Enjoy Life

Lyran starseeds really live their three-dimensional life here on Earth to the absolute fullest. They love to eat, drink, and be merry—anything they can do in a physical dimension that they can't do elsewhere in the galaxy. They tend to be lovers of food who can cook grandiose, delicious meals on their own. They love all types of food and don't bat an eye at dropping a ton of money on an expensive meal. Adult starseeds are known to enjoy drinking spirits and alcohol too.

Lyrans Get the Job Done

Their love of the three-dimensional also extends to doing physical tasks. They don't mind doing hard labor, and, once they begin a job, they will always finish it.

They Are Very Knowledgeable

These particular starseeds can be "know-it-alls." They are extremely astute people who pick up on information very easily. They like to study topics just for fun and are a great addition to any trivia team.

This knowledge serves them well because Lyran starseeds like to be independent. They don't want to be overly smothered by their relationships but rather to maintain their self-sufficient nature. This can lead to problems in their romantic relationships as they don't like to be fussed over or told what to do. For as much as they enjoy the experience of love—especially in its physical form—they have a hard time committing to one person. They just can't help being self-sufficient, autonomous people.

They Are Ambivalent about Space

Unlike the other starseeds we've described so far in this book, Lyran descendants may not feel an affinity for the stars. This is because of the great wars between the Lyrans a long, long time ago. When these occurred, many Lyrans were displaced from their home planets and had to find other places to live. It's believed some of the planets and stars Lyrans originally called home were totally destroyed. So, unlike other starseeds, Lyrans don't feel such a happy longing for a cosmic home in the skies since those homes may not actually exist anymore.

They Don't Always Appreciate 3-D Life

Lyran starseeds in particular have a very different experience on Earth than the rest. While they love being in a three-dimensional body and living a three-dimensional life, they also become frustrated quite easily. They become upset when they can't do things with ease that their soul remembers them doing back on Lyra.

They are actually known to be very clumsy human beings. This is due to their celestial bodies on Lyra being catlike or feline in nature. As we know from Earth, cats rarely fall down without landing on their feet—hence the popular saying. Well, if you can imagine living life with such spatial grace, you can also imagine what a shock to the system it must be to live a clunky existence here.

Chapter 10
Orions

Orions are some of the smartest starseeds in the galaxy. They live within the Orion constellation, one of the most easily recognized in the night sky. They are completely ruled by logic, making them incredibly inquisitive people. They have a strong desire to learn about everything they can, and they make for incredibly successful academics.

WHAT WE KNOW
ABOUT ORIONS

Orions originated from one of the most well-known constellations in our night sky, Orion, also referred to as "the hunter" after its origins in Greek mythology. The stars in the constellation are between 200 and 1,400 light-years away from Earth. The brightest stars in Orion are Rigel, a blue supergiant, and Betelgeuse, a red giant and one of the largest stars in the sky. However, there are six additional stars that shine quite brightly within the constellation: Bellatrix, Saiph, Meissa, Alnitak, Alnilam, and Mintaka, the latter three of which form the asterism (a pattern within a constellation) of Orion's Belt. Despite looking like they are all connected, the stars of Orion are actually quite far away from each other.

The constellation also contains the Orion Nebula, which is visible to the naked eye and makes for spectacular photos (just look online for images of it!). It's located within Orion's Sword and is visible to us as the middle star (despite not being an actual star). Scientists constantly study this nebula for clues as to how stars and planets form and they consider it a "stellar nursery," a place where new stars are born into the universe. In fact, scientists have observed over 700 stars within the nebula at different stages of development.

Where They're From

To find Orion in the night sky, look for the three stars that make up Orion's Belt. It's right on the celestial equator, making it visible to most of the planet. It's best seen between November and March, depending on where you are in the world. Because it's so easily seen by the human eye, many use Orion's Belt to find lots of other stars, planets, and constellations.

The Greek Story of Orion

Like so many constellations in the night sky, Orion also has roots in Greek mythology. As the story goes, Orion was a handsome hunter who was well known for his strength, looks, and many romantic trysts. There are different versions of his life story and how he ended up in the night sky. Some stories say he was the son of the Greek god Poseidon and Euryale, daughter of King Minos of Crete. Others suggest his father was Hyrieus, the son of Alcyone (one of the Pleiades) and Poseidon. Both versions say Orion traveled to the island of Crete, where he met and fell in love with Artemis, goddess of hunting.

In one version of Orion's death, Artemis's twin brother Apollo noted how much time the pair was spending together and did not approve. He'd heard of Orion's womanizing ways and didn't want his sister to be another one of his conquests. While Orion was out swimming in the far-off distance, Apollo challenged his sister to hit a small speck in the middle of the sea with an arrow. Artemis accepted the challenge, unwittingly shooting her bow right into Orion, killing him instantly. In the other version of events, as the two hunters traveled across the country together, Orion boldly declared he would hunt every animal that existed in the world. When Gaea (or Gaia), goddess of the earth, caught wind of this announcement, she sent a giant scorpion to kill him. The scorpion was successful, and Zeus later turned Orion into a constellation—as well as the scorpion that ended his life (the constellation Scorpius).

Their Purpose on Earth

Orions have come to our planet to encourage us to align ourselves with the universe. They do this by choosing to live their lives as human beings who will unwittingly inspire others around them. Some Orions have decided to live their life on Earth in order to work out their karma from previous lifetimes. Orion has seen many wars between the light and the dark in its millions of years of existence, so it's not hard to believe that some beings from this planet feel they need a "do-over" or to try living a better, more loving existence here.

What They Look Like

While there's not a lot of confirmed information about what Orions actually look like, it's believed they have piercing blue eyes. This trait is believed to appear in the human forms of starseeds from the Orion star system. Some have suggested that original Orions appear human-like, while others believe they look like the stereotypical gray aliens depicted in film and TV. On Orion, there are very masculine and feminine races of star beings, which means Orion starseeds can be very masculine, very feminine, or a mix of both energies.

Orions have come to
our planet to encourage
us to align ourselves with
the universe.

TRAITS OF ORION STARSEEDS

Orions may have come to that constellation from other locations in space, and, as such, a lot of diversity is there. If you're a starseed with multiple lineages—which you can discover by communicating with your star ancestors or by taking the quizzes in this book—there's a good chance you've spent time on Orion as well. Orions can choose to live on any of the planets and stars throughout the constellation, and each has a different vibe to it. Depending on where you land, there may be positive beings who want to help humans or the complete opposite. Luckily, the good beings of Orion are superiorly intelligent beings who can keep the bad ones at bay. Their wars have ended and it is now a peaceful place. Due to the polarizing views within the Orion community, many Orions have a duality about them where they can embody both the light and the dark and/or have both feminine and masculine energies within them. Orions are particularly powerful beings who connect with the solar plexus chakra, a human's personal power source.

They Are Very Smart

Starseeds with Orion lineage are astonishingly intelligent and are very fast learners. They also:

- Have an incessant thirst for knowledge that brings them back to their studies over and over again.

- Find delight in libraries and could spend hours browsing through books and picking up on new ideas.

- Could probably get lost in a museum for days (if they didn't eventually have to close).

- Love contemplating the human mind and may be drawn to studies of it.

- Are drawn to the sciences, particularly chemistry, biology, astronomy, and other metaphysical interests. They have a specific knack for understanding these areas of study.

Starseeds of Orion lineage have extremely high standards for learning. They can't stand listening to a teacher who isn't passionate or is just "phoning it in." They're passionate about the act of learning and expect everyone in that setting to be passionate as well. If they respect their teachers, they're known to stick around after class with follow-up questions or to ask for further reading. They have little tolerance for people who act out in classroom settings. They believe the mind is a terrible thing to waste. They usually work best alone or in small groups and tend to dislike large classroom settings. They also make great, caring teachers.

They Have Great Memories

Orion starseeds hold on to and can recall information more quickly than most of us. Their memory tends to be rock-solid, almost as if they can pull anything from their minds at a moment's notice. They can even have photographic memories. This all means they are wise beyond their years (and make excellent trivia partners!). They can come across as "know-it-alls," but they really do know a lot of information, so the title actually fits. They expect others to be the same in this way and can become frustrated with people who don't have intellectual reservoirs like they do. They also hold a lot of opinions and can come off as a bit snobby.

They Are Ruled by Logic

Thanks to their wisdom, Orion starseeds tend to be logic-minded people. Some would say they're logical to the extreme. They look at the world differently than most of us do, usually without any emotions clouding their view. It's not that they don't have emotions; their brains just focus more on the analytical side of life. When faced with an issue, they react to it intellectually instead of emotionally. This trait allows them to be cool in high-pressure situations and in times of danger. They're always reasonable when weighing the pros and cons of a situation and are prepared to call on their survival skills whenever they need to. They have a rationale for every move they make.

They Are Very Curious

These starseeds also have a drive to understand why things are the way they are. Orion starseed children are almost always asking "why?"—to the point of frustrating others. They view everything in life as an educational experience. Traveling to new places means new cultures to learn about, and every time a new person is introduced to them they tend to grill them with questions.

Sometimes the people in an Orion starseed's life will become frustrated with their inquisitive nature. Their questions and comments can be perceived as scrutinizing or criticizing the person they're speaking with. Some people find the constant barrage of questions annoying. If you think you might be guilty of this behavior, you could try softening your language when asking questions, thanking whomever you're talking to for taking the time to explain themselves and/or just letting them know that being curious is in your nature so you might ask a lot of questions. Giving this background ahead of time may allow others to forgive you before they can even become upset. If not, you may also need to learn how to apologize sincerely.

Their Minds Are Always Working

Some Orions are quieter in nature, so they may not always ask questions out loud but instead ask them internally. They tend to overanalyze every bit of their life until they understand every aspect of it. They have a hard time understanding why other people's minds work differently than their own. Unlike many of the other starseeds discussed so far, if an Orion starseed begins to glaze over while they're thinking, they're probably not daydreaming. It's likely they're making mental calculations and analyses, either about an intellectual pursuit or as an attempt to understand their own feelings.

If your mind is always racing, this trait probably resonates strongly with you. Try meditation, breathing exercises, or other methods to help slow yourself down.

They Might Approach Relationships Logically

The Orion focus on logic can lead to relationship troubles. As logical thinkers, they have a low tolerance for their partner acting overly emotionally. It's difficult at times for these starseeds to give the emotional support their partner expects. It's not that they don't care for other people; they just don't operate the same way. When they get into a fight, they tend to focus more on getting to the bottom of why the fight is happening than checking in with the other person. Again, it doesn't mean they don't care about the person—their logical mind just defaults to finding the root of the problem. Their partners can sometimes feel neglected or that their emotions are being ignored. Orion starseeds may have better luck finding other logically minded thinkers to date so they're more likely to see eye to eye.

They're Very Sensitive

While it may seem like Orion starseeds aren't emotional, they're actually very sensitive people. They're easily overwhelmed, especially in large groups, and prefer to avoid large crowds of people. They're also perfectly content spending time alone—it gives them time to learn new things! Starseeds with an Orion heritage are also known to repress their emotions, leading their partners to be confused about their actions or completely clueless about what's really going on inside. Additionally, they tend to have issues with trust and find it difficult to advance a relationship to the next level. For this reason, they can sometimes come across as mysterious.

They Can Have Bold Personalities but Require Validation

It's been said Orion starseeds have strong personalities, but that can vary based on their personality type. Much of this can be attributed to their strong solar plexus chakra, the chakra that controls our personal power. Just like how Orions work with this energy vortex, Orion starseeds are born with an innate connection to this power source. They can harness it at an early age and will at times come across as intimidating to others. They usually have bold personalities and are completely unapologetic for anything they say or do.

That said, Orion starseeds do have a strong need for validation. For some reason, they really want to be respected by others. They will look for compliments or work hard at gaining the respect of someone they'd like to win over. If all else fails, they expect to wow others with their intelligence.

They Are Perfectionists

Orion starseeds can very well fit the mold of a "type A" personality. They always aim for perfection in any task they take on and will do the hard work required to achieve it. They devote as much time as necessary to do the absolute best job they can, sometimes neglecting other needs or responsibilities in the process. Orion starseeds are very detail-oriented and are usually very organized. Even if they appear messy to you, they usually have a method to their mess that works for them. They sometimes have difficulty working with other people, and it usually boils down to knowing they could probably do the task better themselves.

They're Competitive

Starseeds from Orion want to be the very best. They love to win and are incredibly competitive. They strive for first place and will be disappointed if they don't achieve the goals they set for themselves. This is part of why they spend so much time expanding their knowledge—not only because it helps them succeed in life; because it also helps them to win! They want to succeed while they're here on Earth, and they usually do.

They're Witty

Orions can also be successful in winning people over with their humor. They have a dry, witty sense of what's funny and love to tease other people. Just don't be surprised when they switch from humor to their logically minded thinking in a split second.

Chapter 11
Arcturians

Finally, we arrive at the Arcturians. These highly intelligent beings exist within the constellation Boötes, the herdsman. Arcturian starseeds are extremely strong and powerful human beings. They're great speakers and storytellers who are revered by all, yet they maintain a strong desire to not be tied down. They're smart and knowledgeable people who use their communication skills to enact change.

WHAT WE KNOW ABOUT ARCTURIANS

Arcturians hail from the Arcturus star system, a red giant approximately 1.5 times the size of the Sun. It's position in space is relatively close to Earth at around 37 light-years away, and it's believed to be between 7 and 8.5 billion years old. It travels through space at a quick speed alongside over fifty other stars in what's known as the Arcturus stream. Scientists believe this stream of stars first entered the Milky Way over five billion years ago after it collided with another galaxy. However, they believe Arcturus entered our galaxy only 500,000 years ago and that its position within the constellation was much more prominent in ancient times.

Where They're From

Arcturus is the brightest star within Boötes and indicates the left leg of the constellation. It's the brightest star in the northern celestial hemisphere, though it can be viewed from both hemispheres. It's almost always visible throughout the year from different points on Earth. Arcturus is also referred to as Alpha Boötis, a scientific name that indicates it's the brightest star within its constellation.

To find Arcturus in the night sky, follow the handle of the Big Dipper, aka Ursa Major. If you draw an imaginary line from the last star in the Big Dipper's handle to the southeast, you'll land right upon Arcturus. In fact, there's a common mnemonic that goes with these directions: "Follow the arc to Arcturus." It references the arc of the Big Dipper's handle and that you need only extrapolate it out to land at Arcturus. If you continue to follow this same line beyond Arcturus, you'll land at Spica, a star in the constellation Virgo. With the exception of Arcturus, the Boötes constellation is actually quite dim, so it's best to start your search there first. This bright star is easily seen in the night sky and has been observed by humans since ancient times.

The Greek Story of Boötes, the Herdsman

The Greek myth about the constellation of Boötes, the herdsman, has a lot to do with its neighbor in the sky, Ursa Major, which translates to "the greater bear." As the story goes, the Greek god Zeus met a young nymph named Callisto. They fell in love and had a child, Arcas (or Arcturus). When Hera, Zeus's wife, discovered that her husband had not been faithful to her, she hunted down Callisto and turned her into a bear. Callisto spent the rest of her life wandering through the forest until one day she came upon her son and Zeus. When Arcas lifted his spear to strike and kill the bear, Zeus intervened by sending them both up into the sky to live among the stars: Callisto as Ursa Major and Arcas as Boötes, also referred to as "the bear watcher."

Other Cultural Associations of Boötes

Other cultures have different explanations for Arcturus and the Boötes constellation.

- European folklore suggests Boötes (the herdsman) is the opposite of Orion (the hunter) because the two are on opposite sides of the night sky. Orion is seen in the fall and winter, and, when he isn't visible, Boötes is. Their job titles alone provide enough conflict for this rationale to make sense.

- Ancient Romans believed the movement and activity of Arcturus signaled large storms and weather events.

- In ancient India, they referred to Arcturus as Svati, which translates from Sanskrit as "very beneficent."

Arcturus and the World's Fair

In 1933, Arcturus was the main focus of the Chicago World's Fair. The fair's organizers were trying to come up with a splashy way to open the exhibition and recalled that the last time their city hosted a World's Fair was in 1893. Thus, it had been forty years since their last hosting and, since they believed Arcturus was 40 light-years away from Earth at the time, they thought it would be grand if they could somehow use starlight that began its journey to Earth during the previous Chicago World's Fair to open the current one. So they focused telescopes on Arcturus and used its light to trigger photoelectric cells that turned on the floodlights at the fairgrounds. It was a unique and exciting demonstration, though not entirely accurate: Scientists later discovered that Arcturus is less than 37 light-years away from Earth.

What They Look Like

Arcturians are some of the most advanced beings in the galaxy. It's believed they exist on a blue planet that revolves around Arcturus, though scientists on Earth have yet to prove any planets exist in that area. Those who have connected with these beings say they are entirely blue in appearance, just like their home planet. Arcturians' planet is in the fifth dimension, though they can exist up to the eleventh dimension, which means they don't always exist as physical beings. They can appear as energy or light, or incarnate into physical form when traveling to other planets or making contact with humans on Earth.

Their Mission on Earth

Arcturians are believed to be ruled by love and are actively working to help humans on Earth love themselves and each other. Their lessons focus on expelling negativity, fear, and guilt from our lives and exchanging them for truth, love, and light. They teach of self-love and acceptance and are very nonjudgmental. Their planet is said to have been rid of sickness and disease for centuries. They are a people of scientists, explorers, and healers who travel the galaxy to assist other planets in healing themselves. They would love to do the same for all of us on Earth.

Arcturians are believed to be ruled by love and are actively working to help humans on Earth love themselves and each other.

Arcturians' Method of Communication

Arcturians are said to communicate in codes and light language, as so many starseeds are drawn to numbers, codes, and other extraterrestrial languages. Many Arcturian starseeds have said their mission is to encode light within all things on the planet, and they spend much of their time doing so once they learn how.

TRAITS OF ARCTURIAN STARSEEDS

Arcturian starseeds are quite skilled at communicating with others and offering advice and problem-solving ideas.

They Are Strong Communicators

Arcturian starseeds are great communicators. They are extremely tied to their throat chakras, which regulates truth, voice, and overall communication. Given that their home planet is blue and they are known as blue beings, it's interesting that this is also the color of the throat chakra.

These starseeds tend to be extremely expressive people here on Earth. They are incredibly gifted storytellers who end up taking over social situations with their well-told tales. Some have been called "the life of the party." They tend to have opinions about everything and aren't shy about sharing them. They love debating other people who are against their own opinions and they love winning arguments. They are great public speakers and can charm a crowd like no one else.

They're really funny and have a great sense of humor. There's a magnetism about them that draws people into their circle. In fact, they seem to be emitting a specific signal or vibration that draws people to them for a number of reasons.

This is likely due to the fact that, whether or not they intend to or even realize it, they are constantly communicating through their own voice, body language, and the frequencies they emit. Their high vibrations and ties to the cosmic mean they are always putting their thoughts and feelings back into the world, consciously or not. In turn, they are incredibly sensitive to other frequencies, bright light, loud sounds, strong smells, and the vibrations of other people. They don't have a huge tolerance for any of these things and tend to be the people who leave places suddenly because they feel uncomfortable. When this happens, they need to take time for themselves and recharge.

They Give Great Advice

Their magnetism, voice, and the feelings they emit can cause others to be drawn into their lives. They're great at giving advice and people come to them because they seem wise beyond their years. Arcturian starseeds never pass judgment on others and, as such, provide a safe space where people can unload their problems. They're incredibly empathetic and usually know what to say at any given time. Because of this, other people feel safe and accepted around them.

Though they're happy to dole out advice, they will become frustrated with those who ask for their advice yet never act on it. If this happens often enough, they'll eventually refuse to give their suggestions to this person. They can't understand people who don't take their lives seriously, and they really hate it when people whine.

They Have More Acquaintances Than Close Friends

Arcturian starseeds have a protective quality where they will keep the people they love out of harm's way, but they don't tend to have a lot of close friendships. The number of acquaintances they have will generally be greater than the number of friends they have. They're very selective about who they open up to and it takes a lot of time and proving yourself to be considered.

They Keep Their Emotions Inside

They also tend to suppress their emotions and don't like to talk about any feelings they have deep inside. In fact, when conversations come up that are deep in nature or they're asked about something specifically relating to their emotions, an Arcturian starseed will do whatever they can to change the subject or deflect the question entirely. It's just not where they're comfortable. As a result, Arcturian starseeds can be seen as reliable people who "have it all together," and people are subsequently surprised when they discover they aren't totally perfect beings.

They Love Freedom

Like many other starseeds, Arcturian starseeds also feel passionately about expressing their freedom and don't like being tied down. This can manifest as doing lots of world travel, taking lots of vacations, or even moving from town to town. Sometimes they want to experience new things, and changing locations tends to fix that. They get bored easily and don't enjoy feeling like they're stuck in a routine.

If they can't change locations or try new things, they tend to start their own drama in their lives—usually unintentionally—just to generate a little excitement. This can lead to relationship trouble with their friends and particularly with romantic partners.

They're Energetic

Starseeds with Arcturian lineages are likely to be really energetic people who can't sit still. Throughout their day, they never seem to tire and they go from one activity to the next without taking a break. They don't like sitting still or having to be silent—they prefer doing anything else.

Sometimes they're a little "all over the place," but their intense energy can be channeled, and, as such, they can start and complete projects quickly. Sometimes, depending on their personalities, they may start a lot of projects and not finish them, but a mature starseed will generally take on only what they know they can complete. They love the feeling of being accomplished and enjoy checking things off their to-do list.

They Have Strong Personalities

Overall, Arcturian starseeds are seen as strong and powerful people. They may have a strong personality, a strong sense of inner wisdom, or a feeling that they're always right, and oftentimes they are, as these starseeds are very intelligent people with access to more information than they often realize. They tend to recall memories from past lives and can harness the knowledge of the universe with ease once they learn how. They also tend to be claircognizant in nature, meaning they have a psychic knowing inside. This allows them to access information the average person cannot, giving them a greater perspective on the issues at hand. They're expressive people who usually don't think twice about sharing their thoughts out loud.

They Have a Strong Sense of Purpose

More so than other starseeds, Arcturian starseeds feel like they're here on Earth for a specific purpose, usually from a young age. This knowledge can cause distress for those who've not yet figured out specifically why they're here. However, many of them dive into spiritual pursuits that help them discover their true purpose. It's believed they're able to change the energetic frequencies around them and are here to dismantle old and broken systems.

They Like Philosophy and Problem-Solving

Starseeds of Arcturian lineage are inherently philosophical and could wax on at length about human nature or how the mind works. This drive also pushes them to help other people become the best versions of themselves. They are especially skilled at:

- Coaching other people through spiritual and intellectual pursuits.

- Supporting others as they try to reach their goals and learn more about themselves.

- Empowering others—which is why they make great coaches, teachers, and healers.

- Passing along ancient and spiritual wisdom in a way that regular people can understand.

- Recognizing when a system or issue is broken and knowing how to fix it. You may see them proposing new legislation or ideas, constructing new buildings, or changing the way we do things here on Earth.

They are problem solvers who want to fix whatever they can, whether it be a person or a situation.

Chapter 12
How to Meet Your Star Family

All that you've learned in this book may lead you to wanting to get to know your star lineage even better. Perhaps, after taking the quizzes, you want to officially confirm your status as a starseed. Luckily, humans are able to communicate with our star families if we desire. In this chapter, we'll get into the specifics of how to connect with your star families and provide you with suggestions on how to do so.

SETTING AN INTENTION

The first thing you'll need to do in order to meet your star family is set an intention to do so. Just like with your guides and angels, your star family usually won't visit if you don't ask them to. They're supremely intelligent beings who know being visited by them isn't an everyday experience for humans. The last thing they want to do is scare someone! They don't want to give anyone a bad experience or cause them to look at intergalactic visits with stress, anger, or fear. They'll only come to you if you want them to, and even then it may not happen on your first try.

Frame Your Intention in Personal Terms

It's very powerful to set an intention for yourself (rather than putting it all on your star family) since that's much easier to control. You can set an intention like "I am ready to receive messages from my star family" or "I will speak to my star family tonight at eight o'clock." Keep your language positive and definitive. You don't want to say vague things like "I'd like to speak to..." or "I hope to be ready for..." That, by definition, is not an intention. Intentions are specific goals you want to put into action. Anything that isn't positive or definitive won't be as powerful, so take care with the intentions you set.

It's also helpful to add in a bit about what you expect from your communication. For example, you could add the following to your request: "in whatever way will serve me best" or "for the greatest good." It's great to be as specific as you can with your intentions as the universe will generally deliver what you request.

Include a Time Frame

When you set an intention is important as well. If you set an intention without saying when you'd like to actually meet your star family, they might show up at any time. This is not ideal since you'll want to be in a specific mindset and in a very relaxed state. If they come to you at a time when you aren't able to give them the dedicated attention they need, both parties could end up frustrated. It's best to set the intention for a time when you'll be able to receive their messages and communicate with them. Many have found it's good to ask for a visit right when you'd like to meet them, as you will be prepared and ready. You can ask for them to visit you at a specific time in advance, too, but you should make it a priority to be ready and waiting at that time.

Make It Official

Once you've created your intention, you can choose from a variety of methods to officially send it out to the universe. Here are two powerful options:

- Use good, old-fashioned prayer. Simply fold your hands and set an intention for your star family to speak to you using words that resonate with you.

- Write it down in a journal or, even better, write it down and then say it out loud. You can use a mantra for this as well. To use a mantra, come up with a specific sentence that has your goal in mind and repeat it to yourself over and over. Recite the mantra more often the closer you get to when you want to communicate with your star family.

Decide On a Location to Connect

Decide on a location that works well for you. You want someplace where you can be calm, relaxed, and undisturbed as you attempt this communication.

Outside

Some people sit outside at night and look up at the stars for this communication, which can be a beautiful experience. Looking up at your former home as you call on your star family makes for a truly special communication. They may even be able to show you the direction of your home galaxy. Of course, you'll want to make sure you're alone, safe, and in a place where you won't be disturbed. If you have your own backyard, that is the perfect place to make contact.

Inside

If being outside doesn't feel right to you, you'll have just as much luck communicating within the comfort of your own home. If you have a spot where you regularly meditate, use that. If not, it's extremely important to make sure your space is fully prepared. You don't want to be distracted while trying to communicate with your star family, so you'll need to take note of what could disturb you in the room you're using. Do you have a clock that ticks loudly? A faucet that drips and drives you crazy? Neighbors who play loud music at the same time every night? Try to fix or avoid these things if you can. If you live with other people, it's best to ask them not to disturb you at this time. You might even want to lock your door to keep them out. You'll also want to make sure you're as comfortable as possible. If your mind is distracted, you won't be able to focus on the task at hand—clearing your mind so you can receive the communication you desire. Here are some tips for ensuring that your space is comfortable:

- Take a moment to check the temperature of the room. If it's too hot, turn on a fan. If it's too cold, bundle up or bring a sweater to put on if necessary.

- It's also important to check if you're actually comfortable! If you're lying on your bed, make sure it's been made and that you have all the pillows you need. If you're sitting down, try bringing a cushion or meditation pillow to sit on.

- Take notice of any funny smells and burn a candle or some incense if it pleases you.

- If you have crystals that will relax, soothe, or encourage communication, arrange them nearby.

Basically, you should do whatever you can to encourage complete and utter relaxation.

CONNECTING WITH
YOUR STAR FAMILY

Once you've set an intention and found a comfortable spot, it's time to actually connect with your star family. Get excited, because this will be an out-of-this-world experience that will shape your view of the universe and expand your consciousness. You'll be able to tap into their knowledge and ask them all the questions that have been burning inside your soul. But first, you must call them to you. They will not appear unannounced or completely out of nowhere as they don't wish to frighten you. They first need a clear signal that you're ready to meet them.

Know What You Want to Ask Them

Before you get started, try to have an idea of what you hope to obtain from your discussion, as you don't want to waste their time—or yours. Perhaps you want affirmation that you are, in fact, a starseed. Maybe you want confirmation of where you're from. You could ask them about what your mission is here on Earth or what you've come here to do. Maybe you're curious to know who your star family is, or maybe you want to know more about those who are visiting you. You can ask them about something difficult that's happened in your life and for them to shed light on it. If nothing else, you can ask them to impart their wisdom onto you or to share information they believe will help you in this lifetime.

Are you unsure of what to ask your intergalactic family when this transmission happens? Don't stress about it. It's possible they will do much of the talking. They may have messages they want to impart onto you, so you may be able to just sit there and take it all in.

Meditate

One of the easiest ways to communicate with your star family is to tap into them through meditation. As we've discussed, when you are meditating properly, your mind is fully at ease and ready to receive information—or, in this case, communications. If you're not a frequent meditator, practice it for a while before trying to reach out to your star lineage. It's not the easiest task to shut off the incessant stream of thoughts in your mind, yet you must do so in order to establish communication.

What to Say

When you're ready, say something simple like "I now invite my galactic family to speak with me," "I ask for my star family to visit me right now," or "I now ask for my star family, in alignment with the light, to connect with me in whatever way will best serve me and all those around me."

Whatever you say, the intention should be crystal clear and the directions should make sense. It's also key to let them know when the communication is expected, so it's important to say "right now" if you want the transmission to happen at that moment. However, don't fret if you don't say exactly what's written to say in this book: As long as your intentions are there, communication should flow with ease.

One of the easiest ways to communicate with your star family is to tap into them through meditation.

Verify That They Are Good Beings

As with any nonhuman entity you make contact with, you'll want to make sure you're speaking to legitimate, non-dark forces. This warning isn't meant to scare you, but it's important to note that it's possible to communicate with those who do not have your best interests at heart, unfortunately. As it states in spirituality, where there is light there is also dark. And you don't want to be communicating with anyone who isn't of the light.

As such, any being you connect with must be "vetted" first. This process isn't complicated. When you make contact with someone, ask them if they're of the light. When you ask them this, they have to answer honestly. It's strange but true. A dark force cannot pretend to be good or of the light—they have to give truthful answers. The majority of the time, these beings will answer with a "yes." However, if they answer with a "no," you should release them back to wherever they came from. You can do this by saying a simple "no, thank you" or by telling them that you don't wish to connect. You can also take it a step further by saying you only speak with light beings and that they're not welcome back to you. Again, this happens rarely, but it's important to note so you ensure you're speaking with your true star family who will give you the answers you deserve—not someone who will lead you astray.

A simple way of inviting only light beings to talk to you is to ask for that specifically in your intentions and requests. You can call this in by saying "I now ask for my star family in alignment with the light to connect with me right now" or "I invite my galactic team that is aligned with the light to reach out to me."

Be Patient

Keep in mind that, even if you ask to connect with your star family at a certain moment in time, it may not happen right away. A lot of connections with our star families actually happen in dreams because our minds are fully at rest and able to receive information, something some of us may not be able to do during our waking hours. We're able to communicate much more freely in our dreams as we don't have any physical limitations. In dreams, you may be able to travel somewhere with your star family or learn things you wouldn't be able to fully take in if you were awake. When you wake from your slumber, write down everything you can remember from your dreams. If you can't remember it all or have completely forgotten, don't fret—now that you've managed to make contact once, it'll be much easier to do so again!

Record What You Learn

The experiences you have speaking to your interstellar family are truly magical, and you should write them down so you don't forget anything. It's not that you won't remember the transmission itself, but you may have problems remembering exactly what was said to you. It's also not out of the question that you'll receive answers and messages that don't totally make sense to you. Don't write them off; write them down! You'll be surprised at how many things may eventually make sense as time goes on.

Sometimes the messages you're given aren't the ones you expected—or even wanted—but they *are* the answers your star family believes you need. Give them the benefit of the doubt. They traveled indescribable distances to speak with you, so it's not likely that what they said wasn't important. It may make sense to you in a few months, years, or much further into your lifetime.

Making Connections Again and Again

Once you've achieved contact with your star family once, it'll be much easier to connect with them from then on. You may want to take note of the conditions of where you were when it happened and/or what, exactly, you asked in order to bring them to you. A general rule is if it worked once, it'll usually work again.

HOW TO STRENGTHEN YOUR INTUITION IF YOU CAN'T MAKE CONTACT

You may have trouble connecting with your star family—that is a common obstacle for beginners. Even starseeds who are awakened into their previous lifetimes can have problems communicating with their star families. If you've set your intentions, learned how to meditate, prepared your area for the session, and still aren't getting anything, don't give up. There's one area we've yet to discuss as it relates to speaking with your intergalactic relatives, and that's your intuition.

Your intuition has an incredible impact on your ability to receive information from outside your five senses. In the chakra system, your intuition is tied to your third eye chakra, or *Anja* in Sanskrit. This chakra is located on your brow line, right between your eyes. The third eye chakra relates to your inner vision, inner wisdom, and intuition. It's also the key to your clairvoyant abilities. When your third eye chakra is working well, you'll have a wild imagination, clear sense of intuition, an all-knowing disposition, and a sense and feeling of peace. When it's underactive, humans experience judgment, memory loss, and a lack of focus. If it's overactive, you might feel restless and have issues with concentration and anxiety.

This chakra is also how you "see" without your eyes (the ability of psychic sight). When you communicate with angels, guides, and star families, you're usually not speaking to beings in front of you. Instead, you're communicating with them through your mind. It's the mind's imagination, if you will, that experiences "seeing" intergalactic beings during your communication. If you haven't experienced this before, it's like "seeing" with your imagination, but it will feel and look different. Some people can use their psychic sight to see the same way your imagination does, while others see outlines of people and objects in light. It varies for everyone, and if you don't yet know how you "see," get to experimenting! If you have trouble with this inner vision, it's a smart idea to make efforts to see more clearly.

In order to strengthen your inner vision, you can try a number of different methods:

1. **Work on trusting your intuition.** You can do this by repeating a mantra such as "I see clearly" or "I trust my inner vision." You can write it down or simply repeat it over and over again.

2. **Meditate with the goal in mind of expanding your psychic sight.** Your intention for your session will be to improve your inner vision, and meditating with your eyes shut is a simple method of seeing changes in this way.

3. **Use tools of the same color as the third eye chakra—indigo—to assist you in this journey.** People have found that eating foods of the same color can help the body become more intuitive. Try eating grapes, plums, purple carrots, eggplants, and other purple foods to see if it helps. You can also wear the color of the chakra you're hoping to boost. In this case, you'll want to wear bright indigo clothing or jewelry.

4. **Let crystals and minerals aid you in this journey.** Crystals of the same color—amethyst, purple fluorite, lapis lazuli, sodalite, and blue aventurine—are great choices to start with. You can also use moonstone, quartz, sugilite, labradorite, moldavite, and lithium quartz. Hold these in your hands while you meditate or place them around your body in a matrix of sorts. Since you're working with the third eye chakra, it's a good idea to lie down and place them directly onto your forehead for optimal results. You'll be surprised at how you can feel the pulses and vibrations of these powerful stones as they rest atop your chakra.

Your intuition has an incredible impact on your ability to receive information from outside your five senses.

CONCLUSION

Now that you know how to get in touch with your own star family, your overview of starseeds is complete. You've learned what a starseed is, why they're here on Earth, and what their goals are. We discussed the shared traits of starseeds, like being an environmentalist lover of animals with a feeling of homesickness that can't quite be placed, and some of their special abilities, such as clairvoyance, strong intuition, and a variety of other psychic skills. You received an overview of the star system, our galaxy, and what we know about our universe. Finally, we explored several common star families: the Pleiadians, Sirians, Andromedans, Lyrans, Orions, and Arcturians.

Beyond the overview of these topics, I hope you saw yourself reflected somewhere in the pages of this book. Whether you've been inspired to dig deeper into your star lineage or simply felt a bit more understood, the new knowledge you've obtained will allow you to be more empowered and live your true purpose.

Congratulations: You now have a greater understanding of both yourself and the universe at large.

Index

Academics, 55, 56, 159
Age of Aquarius, 21–25
Ancient Egyptians, 20, 123
Andromeda constellation, 136–37
Andromeda Galaxy, 136–42, 172
Andromedans
    appearance of, 140
    compassion of, 143–44
    description of, 20, 87, 135–47
    empathy of, 143–44
    empowering others, 145
    fairness and, 145
    as free spirits, 141
    Greek story of, 137
    as healers, 135, 145–46
    intelligence of, 135, 138, 145
    lineage of, 20, 87
    location of, 136–37
    love of freedom, 142–43
    love of travel, 141–42
    mission of, 138
    origins of, 136–39
    personalities of, 135, 141–47
    purpose of, 138
    relationships and, 141
    self-criticism by, 146–47
    traits of, 135, 141–47
    truth and, 145
    wisdom of, 138, 139, 145
Animals, loving, 47, 50–52, 115
Aquarius, 21–25
Arcturians
    acquaintances and, 179
    advice from, 177, 178
    appearance of, 174–75
    as communicators, 177–78
    cultural associations of, 173–74
    description of, 87, 171–82

empathy of, 178
energy of, 180
Greek story of, 173
as healers, 175, 181
hiding emotions, 179
intelligence of, 171, 180–81
lineage of, 20, 87
location of, 172–73
love of freedom, 179–80
mission of, 175–77
origins of, 172–74
personalities of, 171, 177–82
philosophy and, 181–82
problem-solving and, 177, 181–82
purpose of, 175–77
relationships and, 180
ruled by love, 175–76
as storytellers, 171, 177–78
strong personalities of, 180–81
strong sense of purpose, 181
traits of, 171, 177–82
wisdom of, 171, 180–81
World's Fair and, 174
Astrology interests, 55–57, 127, 133
Astrology signs, 21–22
Auras, seeing, 67–68
Authenticity, 35, 53–54

Big Dipper, 172
Birth, 9–10, 17, 30, 36–37, 55–56,
    88–90
Boötes constellation, 20, 171–73, 172

Cancer, 22
Canis Major constellation, 122
Capricorn, 22
Carrell, Steve, 21
Cassiopeia constellation, 136

Unlock the
Mysteries of Your Soul!

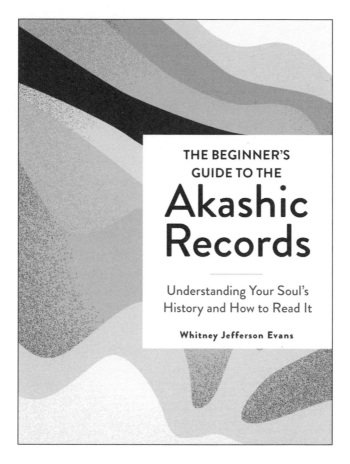

Pick Up or Download Your Copy Today!

adamsmedia
An Imprint of Simon & Schuster
A ViacomCBS COMPANY